LOUISVILLE
MURDER & MAYHEM

LOUISVILLE
MURDER & MAYHEM
HISTORIC CRIMES OF DERBY CITY

KEVEN McQUEEN

THE
History
PRESS

Published by The History Press
Charleston, SC 29403
www.historypress.net

Cover photos courtesy of the Detroit Publishing Company.

First published 2012

Manufactured in the United States

ISBN 978.1.60949.566.4

Library of Congress Cataloging-in-Publication Data

McQueen, Keven.
Louisville murder & mayhem : historic crimes of the Derby City / Keven
McQueen.
p. cm.
Includes bibliographical references.
ISBN 978-1-60949-566-4
1. Crime--Kentucky--Louisville--Case studies. 2. Murder--Kentucky--Louisville--
Case studies. 3. Louisville (Ky.)--History. I. Title. II. Title: Louisville murder and
mayhem.
HV6795.L68M37 2012
364.109769'44--dc23
2011051849

Dedicated to Brayden, Keenan and Delia Pinson

and to the citizens of Louisville, without whose violent and sordid ancestors this book would not have been possible.

Contents

1

The Hanged Butcher's
Alleged Rejuvenation

William Kriel, a rough-and-tumble butcher who lived in Louisville just after the Civil War, might have been as rich as a Vanderbilt had he spent as much time working as he spent drinking and beating his wife, Margaret Evans Kriel. She is described in various reports as being "delicate" and "one of the most amiable of women." The couple had been married fifteen years and had a son. William's butcher shop was on Green Street, and he was well known in town for his honesty. Clearly, he had a private side that few saw.

Early in March 1868, thirty-two-year-old Mrs. Kriel, who was suffering from an illness, decided that she had had enough of her husband's violence. She left him and moved in with her mother on Main Street. William responded with an alcoholic binge of several days' duration that was prodigious even by his degraded standards. On March 5, he dropped by for a visit, which means that he "abused her shamefully," as a press report phrased it. He came back on Saturday, March 7, and demanded to know if she was really going to leave him.

"No, I am not going to leave you," Mrs. Kriel replied, no doubt choosing her words carefully. "The doctor has told me I must go off [to the country] or I will never get well." This was not the answer he sought, and he protested his wife's show of independence by throttling her. A light bulb appeared over Kriel's head—or would have, had Thomas Edison developed it yet. He produced a gun and shot her two inches above the left ear. She died instantly in her elderly mother's arms and went on to a much greater reward than being the spouse of William Kriel.

The drunken butcher sat on the floor and had a first-rate idea: he pressed the gun to his own head and pulled the trigger. A glancing shot tore off his scalp. At this unpleasant juncture, the dead woman's sister, Mrs. Rosa Tolbert, came downstairs to see what all the noise was about. A few weeks before, she had said in confidence that if she had a husband like William Kriel, she would kill him. Somehow, Kriel had gotten wind of the remark, and although the reproof was not unjust, he had been offended. When Mrs. Tolbert entered the room, he shot at her. She ran outside, and he gave chase, firing a second time at the side gate. Luckily, both bullets missed.

Kriel's gun was a six-shooter. Realizing that he had two bullets left, and not wishing to waste them, he shot himself twice more in the head. Thanks to the blind luck of the drunken—or perhaps because Fate wanted to save him for a far worse end—both bullets merely grazed his scalp. Soused though he was, the assassin knew he was in trouble when he saw a crowd gathering outside. He fled, but neighbors followed him and captured him at a pork house on Beargrass Creek. Strange to say, but Kriel appears to have been the only murderer in the entire history of nineteenth-century Kentucky who wasn't threatened with lynching. He was delivered to a jail cell, where it took him over a week to dry out. The two major city dailies, the *Courier* and the *Journal*—it was in the days just before they merged—ran repeated announcements stating that his death from delirium tremens was expected at any time. As late as March 19, twelve days after the murder, it was reported, "The condition of the prisoner is much improved, although he yet exhibits strong symptoms of *mania-a-potu*." During his lucid moments, Kriel said that Mrs. Tolbert had fired at him first and that he was merely returning fire when he accidentally shot his poor, dear wife—after placing the muzzle directly against her head! Needless to say, such statements did not bear analysis.

Margaret's March 9 funeral at the Shelby Street Methodist Church was one of the largest ever held in Louisville. Her mother, who had lost two of her Confederate soldier sons in the recent war, was insensible with grief. Reverend J.W. Cunningham preached a pointed sermon about the dangers of alcohol and wenching and urged husbands to be faithful and kind to their wives. The man who most needed to hear the sermon was unable to attend, however, since he was still gradually sobering up.

When Kriel was at last able to wobble into circuit court on March 18, a reporter said, "[H]e was very sensibly moved at the sight of the mother and sister of his murdered wife, who are to testify against him." He even burst into tears. The reporter speculated that the murderer was suffering from the pangs of remorse; this was possible, but it was equally likely that Kriel realized the testimony of his mother- and sister-in-law would put a noose around his neck.

While Kriel languished in jail, numerous attempts were made to release him on bail, somebody somewhere having decided that it would be a fine thing to let him walk the streets unencumbered. It was decided that he could have bail if he came up with $10,000—in modern currency, nearly $157,000—but to Kriel's chagrin, his relatives refused to risk their savings and property on his behalf, resulting in a chilly feeling between him and his kin that never thawed. When he realized he was not going to get bail, Kriel and his lawyers claimed he was insane. He had never been insane before, just mean, but evidently they hoped to confuse the concepts of insanity and drunkenness.

Kriel's trial lasted four days in January 1869. His victim's mother and sister offered straightforward, unshakable and moving testimonies about what they had witnessed on March 7, 1868. The best the defense could do was to bring in elderly J.W. Knight, who had been a doctor for fifty years. He stated:

> *The liquor used now-a-days not only intoxicates but deranges many who drink it. That has been my experience in this city. In 1812 and 1813 liquor did not hurt men; now it poisons many of them—affects the brain and the whole nervous system. Modern whisky has strychnine and fishberries in it, and deranges the mind. Men under the influence of this liquor, and who have been habitually drunk, are often so affected thereby that they do not know what they are doing.*

Defense attorneys love to utilize the "blame the victim" strategy, but this may be the only known use of the "blame modern alcohol, which unlike the old kind makes men violent" strategy. Kriel's former attorney, Major W.R. Kinney, told the court that he had visited Kriel in his cell the day after his arrest, "and on speaking about killing his wife, he evinced the greatest astonishment." In any situation, "My client was too drunk to know what he was doing" makes a very poor argument for leniency. Perhaps Kriel's attorneys should have entered a plea of self-imposed insanity.

In the face of such a defense, the verdict was a foregone conclusion: guilty, with a recommendation of capital punishment. The date of execution was delayed four times by Governor Stevenson, and many thought Kriel would never pay the ultimate price for his crime. January 21,

1870, was at last chosen as the date when the butcher would be reunited with his wife in the unlikely event that they both went to the same place. The governor was inundated with petitions signed by kindly disposed persons who thought Kriel's life should be spared but whose generosity undoubtedly would have been strained had the same Kriel wanted to marry their sisters or daughters. The condemned man's attorney, General W.I. Jackson, presented the petition to Governor Stevenson and also consumed two hours of that official's valuable time arguing that his client's life should be spared. Jackson received a "patient and respectful hearing," but the governor was undeterred by sentimentality and refused to intervene. No one was surprised much, except Kriel, who genuinely expected his sentence to be commuted.

If Kriel spent his final days reading newspapers, he may have seen a front-page story headlined "A Fearful Gallows Scene" in the January 20 edition of the *Courier-Journal* (by then the papers had joined forces). The article told in graphic detail of a bungled North Carolina hanging that resulted in the guest of honor managing to struggle his way back up onto the gallows platform.

The day before Kriel's scheduled hanging, General Jackson made a motion for a new trial on the grounds that he had just discovered more evidence that the prisoner was insane. His proof must have been unconvincing because the court refused to grant a new trial. When the prisoner realized that the end was really and truly at hand, he telegraphed the governor asking for a few more days to prepare himself for death. The governor must have felt that Kriel had had sufficient time to tend to spiritual matters because no response came.

A *Courier-Journal* reporter was granted permission to visit Kriel during his last night. The prisoner said that he would make his final statements on the gallows. He added that he knew absolutely nothing about his wife's murder—which may well have been true, considering the state of intoxication he had been in when he committed it. Then he availed himself of a lengthy oration in which he complained that the newspapers had prejudiced the community against him, said that the trial had been unfair, implied that witnesses against him had been bribed, admitted that his murdered wife's relatives all hated him for some reason and declared that he couldn't have killed his wife in the manner suggested by the prosecution. By the time he was finished, one would have supposed that everyone in Louisville was out to get him except his lawyers, whom he praised lavishly. He added that he believed in God and hoped that he would meet his Margaret in heaven.

The sheriff obtained all necessary paraphernalia: the rope, the cap and the coffin. The gallows was constructed on Fifteenth Street; at this time, executions in Louisville were still held in public.

The prisoner awoke bright and early on the morning of January 21—proving that he had at least one good habit—and received final visits from his fourteen-year-old son and his brother, George. At 1:30 p.m., Kriel, forty-six years old and dressed in black, walked to the scaffold as ten thousand people scrutinized him for signs of weakness; society then considered failure to "die game" almost as big a disgrace as committing a murder, and of course Kriel would not want to ruin his social standing. A large number of the spectators were women, as always seemed to be the case. During the night, Kriel had become resigned to his fate, and he took his final stroll manfully. He was so calm that several onlookers believed he must have been drugged, a theory denied by his captors. His last request was that his sister receive his hat and pistol—the same weapon with which he had committed the crime for which he was about to be very dramatically punished.

The crowd was well behaved and thoughtful and even appeared to sympathize with Kriel when Reverend Perkins offered a prayer. "That moment was a solemn one indeed," wrote a reporter, "and brought tears to the eyes of thousands in the vast throng there who then, for the first time, truly realized the terrible position of the doomed man." No one was more solemn than Sheriff J.M. Martin, a longtime friend of the man he was about to execute; several of the policemen who accompanied Kriel to the gallows had been his schoolmates. After a couple of prayers from the prisoner's spiritual advisors—kept brief at his request—he was duly pinioned and capped. When the sheriff asked him if he had anything to say, Kriel replied, "No, it would only create talk." At precisely 1:34 p.m., the trap was sprung, and the butcher died instantly. The *Courier-Journal* eulogized him thusly: "Billy Kriel has at last paid the great penalty, but died believing that he had found forgiveness."

The *Courier-Journal* published a letter from a citizen calling himself "W," who complained that executions ought not to be held in public—ought not to be held at all, in fact. He was countered in print days later by "Justice"; their exchange indicates that arguments for and against capital punishment have not changed much in 130 years. The *Courier-Journal* agreed with "W" that hangings should be private but also agreed with "Justice" that "a few fashionable convictions and first-class hangings," especially among moneyed murderers, were necessary to keep society safe.

After the hanging, Kriel's relatives took his remains to the receiving vault at Cave Hill Cemetery to await interment, thus thwarting the intentions of Professor A.T. Keckeler, who had traveled from Cincinnati in hopes of procuring the murderer's head. On January 26, the *Louisville Commercial* published as fact a bizarre rumor that Kriel was not dead; he had only been strangled into unconsciousness by the rope. After he had been coffined and carted off to Cave Hill, so went the story, three men had opened the vault and carried the putative corpse to a "most skillful and learned surgeon." As a dozen medical students watched, the doctor restored him to life with a galvanic battery.

"What have you done? Am I alive?" asked the hanged one.

The *Commercial*'s reporter wrote, "Justice had been satisfied by the public execution, though life returned. Why should [the students] deliver up what had so providentially and wonderfully been restored?" They gave their subject a change of clothes and money. Whereupon the resuscitated, resurrected Kriel made tracks out of the city and disappeared. To add credence to the tale, the *Commercial* pointed out that when a galvanic battery had been applied to the hide of Dave Caution, a Louisville murderer who had been hanged some years before, Caution sat up on the dissecting table, although unquestionably defunct.

Some people took the canard about Kriel's rejuvenation seriously, so the vault was opened. He was still in his coffin, right where the sheriff had left him. It is well that the rumor was unfounded.

2

The Dizzy Blondes Come to Town

If you could go back in time and roam the streets of Louisville in the fall of 1877, you would encounter many Civil War veterans in various states of disrepair, small boys who would someday fight in America's conflict with Spain and unblushing young women wearing the latest scandalous bodices and bustles.

You would be astonished at the murkiness of the city, which would have been illuminated with nothing more powerful than lanterns, fireplaces and gaslights. Thomas Edison would develop the practical light bulb in 1879, but Louisville would not be introduced to its first electric light until November 1881.

If the pervasive darkness did not astound you, the intrepid time traveler, the comprehensive bad odors might. Louisville, like most American cities, had a hit-or-miss approach to sanitation. Dead animals often festered in the public thoroughfares until their own mothers wouldn't recognize them, and huge piles of garbage and horse manure practically became local landmarks. This miraculous stench was also a hallmark of the nice people you would meet. The average person in 1877—not just in Louisville but everywhere— bathed once a week, perhaps less if he could get by without it. There was no air conditioning and no antiperspirant, and all soiled and sweaty clothing had to be laboriously washed by hand.

On the other hand, if your travels through time left you depressed and disillusioned, you could always lift your spirits by walking into any drugstore and purchasing perfectly legal medicinal cocaine with the greenbacks of the correct vintage, which you wisely remembered to bring with you.

In 1877, Louisville was as upstanding a town as any, and more so than most, so a sensation resulted when a vaudeville act called the Dizzy Blondes came to town in November.

Like another musical act that would raise eyebrows ninety years later, the Dizzy Blondes were from Liverpool, England. The troupe originated in the late 1860s. Lydia Thompson was its manager and chief member. After wowing Great Britain, the Blondes opened at Wood's Theater in New York City on November 25, 1868. They immediately became the talk of the town—and New York is a very large and jaded town to become the talk of. Photographs of the Blondes dressed in "the classic garb of burlesque" were hawked everywhere, and their show played to full houses every night for thirteen weeks.

The Blondes, undergoing various personnel changes, took their act on the road and spent the next decade successfully playing in cities across America, including San Francisco and Chicago, where they cowhided Wilbur F. Storey, editor of the *Chicago Times*, not for publishing statements that reflected poorly on their tawdry entertainment, but for describing the dancers and singers as "beefy."

By their tour of November 1877, the act had expanded to include twenty young women, none of them the original Blondes. They played in North Carolina, where their act was decried as "the lewdest and most disgraceful public exhibition ever given in that state." Then the Blondes invaded Bowling Green, Kentucky, where the act was praised by a local paper, the *Pantagraph*. The Dizzy Blondes came to Louisville on the eighteenth and were scheduled to perform at a place called Library Hall the next night. I rather doubt that it was an actual library.

So wicked was the act considered by the standards of 1877 that it is hard to find a newspaper account that will even hint

From the Louisville Courier-Journal *of January 13, 1889. Reprinted courtesy of the* Courier-Journal.

Shocking.

Miss Bonkgtongk (in the box)—Isn't it perfectly shocking how scantily actresses dress nowadays?

From the Louisville Courier-Journal *of February 17, 1889. Reprinted courtesy of the* Courier-Journal.

at just what the Blondes did onstage. It is known that over the years they performed parodies of *Ixion, The Forty Thieves* and *Sinbad the Sailor.* By the time it reached Louisville, the act consisted of songs (evidently, off-color ones) and dances (presumably raunchy ones performed in revealing costumes). These dances included the Parisian minuet, and anything French in those days was considered *ipso facto* morally suspect. Also scheduled were three burlesques with titles guaranteed to interest our heavily mustached, derby-wearing forebears: *The Seven Beauties, or the Dizzy Blondes; The Turkish Harem;* and *One Thousand Virgins.* We can only wonder how obscene the Blondes' routine would now be considered compared to our modern depraved tastes, but I include here three illustrations that depict what passed for a "scantily-clad" woman from the era.

The Dizzy Blondes did their stuff in Louisville on November 19, and on November 20, there was talk of the police closing the show. Chief of Police Edwards explained that he let the show run one night so authorities could see if it lived up to its reputation for indecency. (They sat through the entire show to make sure.) The *Courier-Journal* warned, "The managers of the troupe will be given to understand that if they attempt a performance similar to that of last night they will all be locked up in a station-house on warrants which may be taken out today against them." The paper added, echoing the sentiments of the North Carolina press, "A broader and a more vulgar performance has never been given in Louisville."

As it turned out, there was a second show on the night of the twentieth—a watered-down version, more akin to a joke-filled minstrel show than titillating burlesque—but it was sparsely attended; possibly, the city's sweaty deviants feared being arrested along with the entertainers, against whom warrants had been sworn. The Blondes did not push their luck by risking a third night. They departed for greener pastures: Jeffersonville,

From the Louisville Courier-Journal *of September 25, 1893. Reprinted courtesy of the* Courier-Journal.

Indiana. A local correspondent noted with disapproval the show's popularity there among "mere youths."

A couple of days after their Indiana triumph, the Dizzy Blondes arrived in Cincinnati, a city with a long-standing reputation for prudishness. Astonishingly, the Cincinnatians were so enthusiastic over the Blondes' "terpsichorean perfection" (a sarcastic term for "lewd cavorting") that they played there for several weeks. At last, the slow-moving police closed the show and hauled the Blondes and their managers into court. Their trial was held on January 4, 1878, and the courthouse was as packed as any theater. To everyone's amazement, the judge declared the act was "not sufficiently indecent to punish." The Blondes were acquitted and free to corrupt audiences with their smutty songs and hammy legs anywhere they chose to go.

Flash forward nearly a half century to December 1923. Prohibition was in full force, an unintended boon for moonshiners in Kentucky and everywhere else. The national sensation was affordable radio sets for every home.

Automobile drivers were demanding relief at the pump: the price of gasoline had recently reached a (then) all-time high of $0.28 per gallon. The absurdly low—by our standards—price seems comical until we do the math and realize that Louisvillians were paying the equivalent of $3.53 per gallon in modern currency.

The literary phenomenon was James Branch Cabell's novel *Jurgen*. It was considered obscene in its day but is tame as a kitten by our modern standards—such is the spirit of the age—and the once controversial book is now both unread and unreadable.

Louisville's Kentucky Theater had been completed in 1921. Some of the biggest movie hits of 1923 were comedies: Buster Keaton's *Our Hospitality* (with a plot set in antebellum Kentucky) and two starring Harold Lloyd, *Safety Last* and *Why Worry*. Squeaky clean Mary Pickford was the most popular film actress in America, but moviegoers who desired to see skin could always opt for something featuring Clara Bow.

In 1923, the city was home to a tobacco factory that manufactured a brand of cigarettes called Clown. Presumably, Louisvillians in need of a nicotine fix would mutter such things as, "I'm running low on Clowns! I'm craving a Clown! If I don't get me a Clown soon, I'm gonna go crazy!!!" The product's delightfully bizarre ad campaign featured illustrations of clowns smoking while doing circus stunts. The slogan was "The fun is in the smoke"—making one wonder what exactly the ingredients in Clown cigarettes were. (In 1924, the manufacturer would sponsor a baseball team called the Louisville Clowns, a name that probably did not instill dread in the hearts of its opponents.)

The intrepid time traveler in search of thrills could no longer walk into any Louisville drugstore and legally buy cocaine in 1923, but there was no shortage of back-alley peddlers willing to sell it illegally—and also heroin, morphine and moonshine.

And on December 9, in a moment that probably provoked feelings of déjà vu among the city's older citizens, the Louisville police broke into the Gayety Theater and closed down an act called the Step Lively Girls on the grounds that it was obscene. The *Courier-Journal* explained, "Capt. E.A. Larkin, chief of detectives, saw them yesterday afternoon and didn't like their step—or the way they did it." Major Ben Griffin, assistant chief of police, said, "The show is dirty. It's not what they do, it's the way they do it." As was the case back in 1877, the press declined to record what the Step Lively Girls did onstage that was so controversial, although the *Courier-Journal*'s theater columnist hinted that the problem was their dancing: "The police objected to the 'wiggles' of the girls although it was whispered that the performance was not quite as 'raw' as it was last week."

The ban lasted only a day or two, and by December 12 the Step Lively Girls were back onstage at the Gayety, stepping lively as ever. The Dizzy Blondes who had scandalized Louisville back in 1877—many of whom were respectable grandmothers by 1923—may have read in the papers about the closing and enjoyed a private, nostalgic giggle.

3

Chestnut Street's House of Horrors

In the years just before the Great Tornado struck Louisville, there stood a squat, unimpressive three-room cottage at 1922 West Chestnut Street. In that cottage lived a family consisting of Mrs. Alice Brownfield; her three-year-old baby, Harold; her brother, William Bruner; and, at the head of the family, Charles B. Brownfield, a clerk with red muttonchop whiskers like those favored by former president Chester A. Arthur. To neighbors, Brownfield seemed to be a calm, steady family man—which only goes to prove that we can never tell what is going on inside someone else's head, and likely we would be frightened if we could.

Thirty-year-old Charles was the son of Justice Brownfield and had worked for various Louisville companies as a clerk or traveling salesman since the age of fourteen. Around 1882, while on a business trip to Elizabethtown, Hardin County, Charles was smitten with Alice Bruner, a pretty girl two years his junior who happened to be riding on the same stage for Louisville. They were married at Father Lawler's church in Louisville on the same day they met.

Their marriage appeared to be happy. However, there were warning signs that seem obvious in retrospect. Mrs. Brownfield had received $5,000 from the sale of her father's estate in Washington, Indiana; considering that this sum would be the equivalent of over $116,000 in modern currency, the Brownfields could have been set for life had they been wise with it. But the money disappeared quickly. Mr. Brownfield developed extravagant tastes; he lived beyond his means and therefore had to continue scratching out

Charles Brownfield. *From the* Louisville Courier-Journal *of November 5, 1887. Reprinted courtesy of the* Courier-Journal.

a precarious living. In September 1887, when the windfall money was exhausted, the Brownfields moved into the squalid, sparsely furnished cottage on West Chestnut Street. Charles was barely able to keep his immediate family afloat, and some of his friends said that he resented it deeply when his brother-in-law, William Bruner, whom he considered "worthless," moved in with them.

Around the same time Charles moved his family into those less-than-luxurious surroundings, he began working for Rosenberg, Flexner and Company. Although he had earned a reputation for scrupulous honesty, he fell into the gambling habit—perhaps in a desperate bid to recoup his losses and put his family back on easy street. He played poker but was not good at it and lost considerable amounts, which he would try to regain by playing the lottery. He was highly superstitious, and it was said that he based his lottery number choices on his dreams. (This is not recommended.)

Neighbors who saw Charles on the night of Thursday, November 3, 1887, later remarked that he seemed normal and not agitated. At 6:00 a.m. on Friday, Charles's brother Henry stopped by the house to say hello, as was his habit. Charles stepped out and gave a brief morning greeting. He did not invite his brother inside.

Hours passed; nobody exited the house. Number 1922 West Chestnut was as silent as the tomb. Shutters and doors remained closed. Despite being an autumn day, smoke merely curled up from the chimney and then was altogether extinct. The Brownfield family's horse stood waiting for its master; when no rider appeared after the accustomed time, it became visibly nervous and restless. Neighbors passed the house on the way to and from work, each with his or her own immediate concerns, and nobody stopped to add up the clues and consider that something unpleasant might have taken place.

At last, late in the morning, Alice Brownfield's mother, Mrs. M.A. Bruner—who was noted in the neighborhood for continuing to wear the fashions of thirty years before—paid a social call. She was accompanied by Alice's sister, Mrs. Mary Seawright. Mrs. Bruner knocked on the locked front door. No answer. She rattled the doorknob. Still no answer. Well, this *was* peculiar! The women asked neighbors if they knew where the Brownfields were. No one had seen them in several hours.

Alarmed, Mrs. Bruner and Mrs. Seawright returned to the cottage and found every door locked, as well as all the windows except one, which also had an

Alice Brownfield. *From the* Louisville Courier-Journal *of November 5, 1887. Reprinted courtesy of the* Courier-Journal.

open shutter. Peering in, Mrs. Bruner saw a lamp burning with false cheer on the mantel. She opened the other shutter and saw women's clothing scattered on the floor. She saw something else, too, near the window and only eight inches from her face. And so strange and unexpected that it took her several seconds to realize what it was: a human body swinging limply in a doorway, suspended from a noose tied to a transom beam. She did a double take. The form slowly turned in the air, revealing the distorted facial features of her son-in-law.

Mrs. Bruner fell back against a fence and emitted shrieks that were probably audible in New Albany. Of course, Mrs. Seawright had to look for herself, and her terrified cries attracted a neighbor, Mrs. Wallace, who had a key to the house. The three women opened the door and took an ill-advised tour of the house, accompanied by a crowd who wondered what the commotion was all about.

(The *Courier-Journal* ran illustrations showing various rooms and a diagram of the floor plan and location of such details as the doors, windows and furniture; a reader with a florid imagination can re-create what this multitude saw as they ventured from room to room.)

The fragrance of recent death filled the air when the nosey neighbors entered the house. The crime scene—or rather, scenes—were notable for the copious amounts of blood spattered on every surface, including walls, floors and bedding.

In a bed in a corner of the middle room lay both Mrs. Brownfield, with a "calm peaceful expression on the waxen [facial] features," and baby Harold, their white nightclothes turned red with blood. Alice had been brained with the blunt end of a hatchet, and both had their throats cut. Their positions indicated that they died instantly in their sleep. Her clothing had been thrown on the floor, but otherwise everything was in its proper place. Charles Brownfield dangled in the doorway that separated this bedroom from the kitchen. His feet were only three inches from the floor. He wore a red flannel shirt and light-colored trousers and had not shaved in two or three days. A reporter who saw this nameless horror up close and personal wrote, "The face of the wretched murderer was distorted with an expression of extreme agony, and the eyes bulged almost from their sockets. The lips were thick and swollen." Mr. Brownfield's plan to break his own neck quickly had not come to pass, and he had strangled to death. He had eighty cents in his pocket.

The curious throng stepped through this door and into the kitchen (they must have pushed Mr. Brownfield's body to the side like a ghastly curtain). Here they found body number four: the detested brother-in-law, William Bruner, lay in a blood-soaked bed near the stove. Like Alice and Harold, his throat had been cut, but with such violence that he had nearly been beheaded. William's attacker had also caressed his noggin with a hatchet. A reporter observed that his "limbs were twisted in unnatural positions, and it appeared as if the victim had made a struggle for his life." This theory was strengthened by the fact that, unlike in the bedroom, there were signs of disorder, as though the victim had defended himself in his final moments.

After the bystanders had feasted their eyes on the sights in the cottage, the coroner and the police arrived. The authorities found so many interesting things there, such as a razor and a hatchet on the floor beneath Brownfield's rotating remains; they were the tools by which he had dispatched his loved ones, and also his brother-in-law, to the Promised Land. After Coroner Miller cut Brownfield down, he discovered a minor cut on the neck of the deceased. Brownfield had intended to commit suicide by cutting his throat, just as he had done to his family members, but had chickened out and resorted to the rope instead.

A washbasin contained bloody water. There was little food in the house, but a few crusts of bread were on the kitchen table. One in particular bore teeth marks and was heavily dusted with a name brand pesticide called

Mrs. Brownfield and baby. *From the* Louisville Courier-Journal *of November 5, 1887. Reprinted courtesy of the* Courier-Journal.

Rough on Rats. Investigators found half a box of the poison in a chair, and more was found on the floor. A letter on a mantelpiece revealed the unhappy state of Brownfield's mind at the end of his life:

> TO WHOM IT MAY CONCERN.—*I, Charles B. Brownfield, murdered my dead wife and baby; also W.F. Bruner, my brother-in-law. I killed my wife and baby because I was tired of life, and I did not want them left in the world penniless and no one to care for them. My cause for being tired of life is gambling. Now let my brothers and friends take warning. I killed W.F. Bruner because I did not think he was fit to live and now I will make an attempt on my life, so goodbye, my father, brothers, sisters, friends and relatives. All take warning. Good-bye.*
> CHAS. B. BROWNFIELD.
> *Time about 6:30 A.M.*

The reader will note that even in his concluding despondency, Brownfield's inner clerk emerged. He started with a formal, businesslike salutation, perhaps due to force of habit, and ended with the approximate time he dipped pen in inkwell to write his suicide note.

Based on the forensic details, police were able to re-create a likely scenario for Charles Brownfield's mental breakdown. Sometime the previous night he stunned his wife with the hatchet and then slit her throat and the baby's; afterward, he treated his brother-in-law to the same fare in the kitchen, probably after a struggle. Then, he washed his hands in the basin and waited several hours, doing who knows what in the increasingly chilly cottage. Early in the morning—interrupted at some point by a brief visit from his unwitting brother—Charles wrote his suicide note, after which he attempted to poison himself with Rough on Rats. Perhaps fearing the agony that was certain to follow, he made a tentative, ineffective cut on his throat and then decided to stop playing around and hang himself in the doorway. Brownfield's horse and buggy stood at the ready, complete with a valise containing his clothing, as though he had intended to flee after butchering his family and then chose to kill himself due to fright or remorse.

After the police and coroner had accomplished their purposes, the undertakers came to prepare the bodies. In Anno Domini 1887, corpses were

Will Bruner's bedroom. *From the* Louisville Courier-Journal *of November 5, 1887. Reprinted courtesy of the* Courier-Journal.

usually made presentable for burial not at a funeral parlor but in their own homes. A half dozen neighborhood women volunteered to help Undertaker Cralle. He removed the rope from Brownfield's neck, dressed him in a "new suit of striped Scotch cloth" and laid him out in the front room for public display. He stitched up the throats of Alice, the baby and William Bruner with hemp. Mother and child were placed in the middle room—a *Courier-Journal* reporter noted, bizarrely, that "both made beautiful corpses"—as the assisting women wept, sympathized and cooed that they looked as though they were merely asleep, which seems to be the default compliment people always have for the dead.

Before the day was over, the three Brownfields and Mr. Bruner would be placed on adjacent biers in the front room. The undertaker applied his restorative arts well; even Mr. Brownfield looked presentable, despite his blue and swollen lips and protruding tongue. However, William Bruner's countenance bore "a frightened, troubled look." Perhaps because of this, the four corpses' faces were covered with white linen. Naturally, when the front door was opened at 5:00 p.m., a long line formed consisting of friends, neighbors and relatives of the victims but also unrelated persons of every conceivable race, gender, religion, occupation, social stratum, political affiliation, astrological sign and hat size who just wanted to sneak a peek. A couple of burly policemen kept the line moving.

A crowd of such enormity materialized the next day to see the coffins carried out of the house that the crush of sightseers nearly collapsed a fence. Some low comedy unfolded when a hearse stopped nearby; it was an object of rapt attention until the throng realized that it was there to pick up the body of someone in the neighborhood who had died of natural causes. It was only the hearse of a nobody, rather than a victim of Louisville's latest shocking tragedy, so the scornful crowd regarded it with the contempt they felt it deserved.

All that was mortal of the victims was taken to St. Louis Cemetery. Charles Brownfield thought his troubles were ending when he tied the rope around his neck and jumped off a washstand; it may well be that his troubles were just beginning, and on a cosmic scale. The family was Catholic, and the church refused to provide a ceremony for the wholesale murderer of himself and his family. Perhaps it could be contended that if anyone on earth desperately needed the sympathetic gesture of the final rites, that person was the late Charles B. Brownfield of Louisville, Kentucky.

The murderer's suicide letter appeared to explain very little, and the city speculated for weeks about what had been the *real* motive of the massacre.

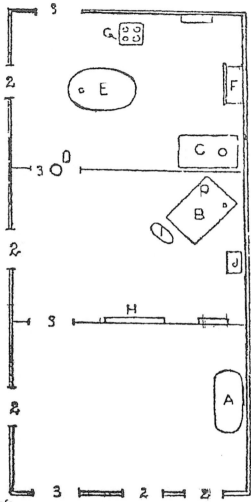

A. Sofa
B. Bed where mother and one child were found
C. Bed where brother-in-law was murdered
D. Body of Brownfield hanging in the doorway
E. Dining table on which was found a box of Rough on Rats
F. Wardrobe
G. Kitchen stove
H. Fire-place
I. Baby carriage
1. Trunk
2. Windows
3. Doors

Map of the Brownfield cottage. *From the Louisville* Courier-Journal *of November 5, 1887. Reprinted courtesy of the* Courier-Journal.

Had he been an alcoholic? His brother Joseph swore that Charles did not drink to excess. Was Brownfield insane? Neighbors thought he had seemed normal on the evening of the murders. Had there been marital difficulties? Extensive investigation revealed no hint of adultery on either his part or the part of his wife.

Joseph Brownfield found it difficult to come to grips with the fact that his brother was a mass murderer. He suggested that the crimes must have been committed by somebody else—exactly whom, he had no idea. There was a wee flaw in his theory. Charles had written a confession letter and hanged himself. Joseph performed logical acrobatics by rationalizing that the real murderer might have killed the family, drugged Charles and then hanged him in order to frame him and make it look like suicide. The letter was a forgery, he declared; the handwriting looked nothing like his brother's. He suggested that the motive might have been robbery—forgetting, it would appear, that Charles had been as poor as Job's turkey.

Another brother, Henry Brownfield, believed that Charles had killed William Bruner first and then his wife and child. He thought Brownfield and William Bruner must have argued while the former was in the act of breaking up coal for the kitchen fire and hence had a hatchet conveniently in hand. After killing Bruner, Charles was contrite and horrified, or so Henry thought. He was certain to go to jail and lose his social standing. Rather than subject Alice and his infant son to the humiliation of having a jailbird husband and father, Charles decided the humane thing to do was to slaughter them as well. Other family members, noting Charles's tenderness of heart and devotion to his family, could only believe that he had fallen victim to temporary insanity. They recalled how horrified he had been when he had read in the papers of the murder of a maid, Jennie Bowman, which had rocked Louisville a few months earlier. They claimed that his so-called gambling addiction had been exaggerated and that he only played the lottery once in a while and never to excess. In a further display of grim determination to avoid facing reality, the family also stated that, despite appearances to the contrary, Charles had been financially well off and therefore could not have murdered his relatives due to despondency wrought by poverty. He had, presumably, moved into the dump at 1922 West Chestnut because he admired the view.

The most absurd theory was that Brownfield had clubbed his family and slit their throats and then had written a letter, poisoned, cut and hanged himself *while in his sleep*. Family members said that the man of the house had been a sleepwalker. On one occasion when Brownfield was a young man, he had gone on a visit to Hodgenville, Larue County, and there had arisen in his sleep and tramped a considerable distance through the countryside. He awoke only when he walked into a pond. The murder-by-somnambulism theory died a sorry death when it was recalled that Brownfield's brother Henry had paid a visit to the house around the time the slayer had been composing his farewell note, and Charles had been quite awake when he answered the door.

The wealthy Brownfields hired a private detective to find out who *really* murdered Charles and his family and, not incidentally, to save the dead man's reputation. Despite a promise that "interesting and hitherto unknown facts will be given to the public in due time," nothing was ever heard of these findings. It is to be presumed that there were no findings and the Brownfields wasted their money.

In the end, the truth seemed to be exactly what Brownfield had stated in his miserable final letter. He had been humiliated by his poverty and had lost great sums by gambling. It was shown that he had lost $5 in the lottery recently; in 1887, that would have been an average person's weekly wage. Brownfield had gone on a trip for Rosenberg, Flexner and Company shortly before his death, and some speculated that he had frivoled away his employers' money at the card table. Worse, he may have been an embezzler. The day after the massacre, William Burchall revealed that he had paid a $70 debt to the firm through Brownfield—but it never received the money. On November 10 came the news that the company had indeed found a shortage of at least $215 in Brownfield's accounts. That would be equivalent to nearly $5,000 in modern currency. There may have been much more money missing, since this announcement was made before the company had examined even half of Brownfield's papers.

Soon after the butchery, the house at 1922 West Chestnut was cleaned, renovated and put on the market. Many persons were heard to remark that they wouldn't live in such a charnel house even for free, but at last the owner rented it to a young man named George Shafer and his wife. The neighbors welcomed the Shafers into the community by telling them about the horrifying, ghostly things they had seen and heard there. One neighbor said to Mrs. Shafer, "Oh, I wouldn't live here for anything! Are you not afraid? Why, every time I looked at that door I should imagine I saw that man hanging there!" Mrs. Shafer replied with admirable pluck that if she ever saw a man hanging in the doorway, she would twist the body "to see how many times he would turn around." In the end, well-intentioned souls made such a nuisance of themselves that Mr. Shafer considered posting a sign in the yard reading, "No Ghosts. No ghost-hunters wanted."

4

Carrie McBride,
the Pugilistic Prostitute

One could write a lengthy monograph on the history of prostitution in Louisville, or one could write a biography of Carrie McBride, the city's most infamous streetwalker in the latter half of the nineteenth century. Her life serves as a microcosm of the wretched lives endured by most members of her class.

She was born Sarah J. Williams in Lawrence County, Illinois, around 1858 to a family of wealthy farmers who spoiled her when she was a child and gave her a good education. But in 1875, when she was seventeen, she abandoned her loving family and went to Jeffersonville, Indiana.

Sarah lived a respectable life there—at first. But one fateful day, she crossed the river with some friends and went on a picnic near Louisville. Late that night, the others returned to Indiana, but Sarah got lost and wandered the streets. The police, assuming she was a lady of ill fame, locked her up for the night. Something about the experience unhinged her, and she became, in fact, what she had been mistaken for, changing her name to Carrie while on the path to perdition. She also decided to remain in Louisville because the place appealed to her. It is hard to escape the politically incorrect conclusion that all the unpleasant events that happened in Carrie's life afterward occurred because she *chose* to live that sort of life despite her many advantages.

For the next twenty-one years, she plied her trade mainly in Louisville. At first, she lived in a tough brothel, the Bowles House on East Market Street. She was one of the more attractive inmates, and many fistfights occurred over her personal wares. She lived temporarily with a man named

McBride, and though they never married, she was called by his surname the rest of her life.

Carrie McBride became addicted to drink, and as her looks faded, she moved down the social scale—or what passed for a social scale among Louisville's lowlifes. From the Bowles House she moved to the even worse American House at Floyd and Jefferson Streets; from there, in 1879, she moved to a predominantly black neighborhood, where around 1883 she married a riverboat worker named Ed Duncan. Why Duncan thought marrying a prostitute would improve his lot in life is a mystery, but his unblushing bride was to make him miserable in the years ahead. A scant six months after the nuptials, she abandoned Ed and "renewed her old habits." The couple was destined to reunite and split often.

McBride was not only the city's most notorious prostitute but also its noisiest and most quarrelsome. As years passed, she became tough as a pine knot and homely enough to quell a riot. She was hauled before the police judge on charges such as disrupting the peace between five and thirty times every year. She was as adept with her fists as a real-life Popeye—and also like the cartoon sailor, Carrie had one eye fewer than she was born with—and any time she was drunk, which was most of the time, she would pick fights at the slightest provocation. She would thrash her husband, rival ladies of the evening, friends, customers and total strangers. In this fashion, she acquired a string of unladylike nicknames, including "One-Eyed Carrie" and "Double-Fisted Carrie."

Policemen dreaded crossing Carrie's path, as the encounters usually were not at all to their advantage. It often took four able-bodied officers to subdue her and take her to jail. Part of Carrie's problem—not to mention society's—was that judges seemed reluctant to give her the punishment she richly deserved and instead doled out light sentences. She was fined countless times, and whenever she couldn't pay, she spent time in the Louisville workhouse. It will be instructive to list a few of Carrie's greatest hits, so to speak:

☛ On May 11, 1889, Carrie went to court for shellacking one Mary McBride in a fight. She was fined $20 and placed under a $1,000 bond for a year. Afterward, she left the city for Carrollton.

☛ On October 1, 1889, Carrie got into a brawl on Lafayette Street with Lena Hoke and Eliza Stone, during the course of which McBride threw a lamp at Stone's face—while the lamp was still lit. Stone suffered several deep gashes, and someone clubbed McBride over the left eye with a stick.

☛ On March 25, 1890, Carrie entered a brothel on Lafayette Street and singlehandedly whipped everyone inside and threw them out onto the street. She and her husband had been kicked out of the house by the inmates three months previously, and she was angered when they refused to let her inside to collect her furniture. This deed was a milestone for Carrie, since it resulted in her 200th arrest within five years. Two days later, the Great Tornado struck Louisville, and to some who had faced McBride's wrath, it might have seemed like a sweet diversion.

☛ In December 1895, Carrie was sentenced to a year in the workhouse. Florence Love of the Flower Mission charity persuaded the judge to let Carrie out. She was arrested again before nightfall and spent Christmas in the pokey.

☛ On January 18, 1896, Carrie outdid herself by being arrested on two charges on the same day: one for being drunk and swearing in public on the corner of Second and Green Streets, and the other for disorderly conduct, on a warrant sworn out by a man who lived on Lafayette Street.

☛ On January 28, 1896, she received a one-year sentence on an undisclosed charge, but after only three months she was freed to commit more mischief.

Early in 1888, Carrie was found lying in a gutter, nearly frozen to death. She stayed in the hospital until she thawed out, and then her need for alcohol and opium took over and she fled to go on a spree. She ended up riding in a hack with an equally drunken man, who kicked her out onto the cold street when the horse approached her residence. She was deemed too badly bruised to go to the workhouse and was shipped back to the hospital. When she tired of that, she checked out and returned to her dwelling place: an attic apartment at 105 East Jefferson Street, filthy, badly ventilated, low-ceilinged and poorly furnished (a reporter noted that the furniture seemed to consist largely of empty whiskey bottles, dirty plates and a heap of "fetid garments"). In these unpromising surroundings, she stretched out on the pallet that served as her bed, a very ill woman. On March 3, the newspapers announced that the notorious Carrie McBride was dying of tuberculosis.

Carrie did not die, however—not by a long shot. Three months later, she arose from her putative deathbed and stabbed her husband, Ed Duncan, three times in the neck with a bread knife when he protested her insistence on returning to streetwalking. Specifically, she had returned to their home with a new customer, and Duncan refused to leave. (By this point, Carrie had a prematurely aged appearance due to her hard living, abuse of alcohol and drugs, illness and constant fighting. It is hard to see how she continued to attract customers, but some men must have been aroused by the loud, drunken, bellicose, two-fisted, one-eyed consumptive type.) After cutting her husband, Carrie and her new companion fell asleep on the floor in a drunken stupor. Ed survived his injuries, and Carrie was arrested. She was sent to the workhouse for a couple of months and was released on August 11—hardly any punishment at all considering the seriousness of the charge. The day Carrie was released, she was arrested for stabbing Duncan in the neck again, this time because he refused to give her fifty cents.

At the end of 1888, the press announced that Carrie had left Louisville forever and would instead grace Cincinnati with her presence. The news, which came on December 20, was considered an early Christmas present by the entire city police force, which thought it would no longer have to fear her beatings. But the joy was premature: Carrie was back in town by April 14, 1889, when two citizens found her lying in the street at Congress Alley. She was arrested without incident and placed in a cell, but when she sobered up she claimed someone had stolen her diamond pin. Officer Jake Haager expressed healthy skepticism about her claim, and the fight was on. It was declared a draw when the dust settled.

In an attempt to reform and salvage her life, in November 1891, Carrie left Louisville for the town of Henderson but came back in January 1892. She announced her arrival by applying for aid at the Charity Organization. She said she didn't like Henderson because "everybody [was] a-dyin' of diphtheria" there. She paid Louisville a dubious compliment by saying she returned because she loved the city so much.

Speaking of the Charity Organization, McBride was not utterly forsaken by the better elements of society. Many efforts were made to lift her from the gutter. The aforementioned Florence Love took her to the Home of the Friendless several times and tried to reform her, but all attempts to reform Carrie proved to be the failure of the age. Her abiding love of alcohol overruled everything else, and she seldom stayed at the mission for long.

We must all face the end sometime, even persons with as much spirit as Carrie McBride. Characteristically, she chose the date and method of her own passing, and the last few months of her existence were as action packed as the years that preceded them. By 1893, Carrie was living with Ed Duncan in the back room of a squalid dump at 305 Pearl Avenue. On

Carrie McBride's funeral. Note swanky charity coffin. *From the* Louisville
Courier-Journal *of July 15, 1896. Reprinted courtesy of the* Courier-Journal.

June 6, 1896, she was arrested for public intoxication. It proved to be
the last of her many, many arrests. In her degraded mental and physical
state, she suffered from delirium tremens, and she screeched the night
away in her cell. Turnkey Alf Davis told a reporter who inquired about
the unholy racket:

Oh, that's Carrie McBride. Just drunk again, that's all. She sees snakes and things sometimes. I remember she was in here once and imagined two big turtles were fastened on her. She said one clawed at her back and another at her breast, and that they were fastened on with a strap. After she got sober she told me that she was sure I and Jailer Watts had a big, long snake which we used on the prisoners. She said Col. Watts guided its head through the bars while I shoved it by the tail; but she said those turtles just scratched and became frantic when the snake got near them.

On the morning of July 13, Carrie decided that enough was enough and ended her life by drinking two ounces of digitalis, which she had been taking for a heart condition. Her husband thought she was just kidding but found her dead on her mattress hours later. He should have suspected that something was up since she spent her last days boozing heavily but had remained out of character by being quiet and not getting into a single brawl. The pitiable creature was only thirty-eight years old when she died.

The ladies of the Flower Mission—who had attempted repeatedly to help Carrie while she was alive—now paid for her funeral, which was held in the Star Baptist Church in the seedy area of Louisville known as "the Chute." Her coffin was a $1.60 pine box, appropriately painted red, provided by the city. The church was packed with people, more of them spectators than mourners. One of them made the following remarks about the corpse: "She looks jes' beautiful. I seen her. She had on a white satin dress, with jes' beautiful bows of satin ribbon, an' red an' white flowers an' a bunch of flowers in her crossed hands. She looks jes' beautiful." This funereal finery came courtesy of the Flower Mission. Outside, according to a reporter who attended, "on the pavement men and women were cursing and laughing with reckless abandon."

There is an old southern superstition that holds that if you speak the name of a dead person, that person's spirit will know it and will be gratified. In case the superstition is true, I urge the reader to speak aloud the name of Carrie McBride and give her ghost some small measure of happiness.

5

Murder Will Not Always Out

On August 4, 1892, a crime occurred in a staid home in Fall River, Massachusetts, that soon was on the minds of all Americans: the hatcheting of wealthy Andrew and Abby Borden. The murders were widely believed to have been committed by one of the family's daughters, Lizzie, but were never officially solved. Barely more than a month later, another double homicide unfolded in Louisville. The case received less national attention than the Borden murders—but it certainly made a splash in Louisville.

It happened in a brothel located above Vince Spaninger's produce store at 339 Second Street, in the city's red-light district. On the night of Thursday, September 8, the occupants of the house—other than the customers—were Emma Austin, age forty, proprietor; one of her prize employees, Eugenia Sherrill, twenty-six years old and blond; Mrs. Austin's eleven-year-old son, Lloyd; Rachel Jackson, who did laundry at the bordello (but what a thankless job that must have been); and Mrs. Jackson's small daughter, Lillie. It was said that a young man came to the place to visit the highly attractive Eugenia Sherrill. Somebody sent out for twenty cents' worth of ice cream. All of the house's denizens partook of it, to no ill effect.

The next morning, little Lloyd Austin complained that he felt sick, but he left for school anyway at his mother's insistence. Mrs. Austin made breakfast. Should anyone be curious about the typical morning meal of the nineteenth-century demimonde, it consisted of batter cakes, coffee, cantaloupe and preserves. Only Mrs. Austin and Mrs. Sherrill ate.

Within minutes, the two were sicker than they ever could have imagined. They bolted from the table, stricken with chronic vomiting and diarrhea. Their cries of misery were so loud that another inmate of the house, Mrs. N. Johnson, investigated. (Mrs. Johnson was from Cincinnati and later would claim that she was staying in Louisville briefly on business; a friend had secured the room at Mrs. Austin's for her a couple of weeks before, and she had had *no idea* at first that she had been rooming in a "house of assignation." She did not explain why she chose to stick around after she discovered the truth.)

Mrs. Austin. *From the* Louisville Courier-Journal *of September 11, 1892. Reprinted courtesy of the* Courier-Journal.

Dr. Brennan was called in about 8:45 a.m.—doctors still made house calls then, even to houses of ill fame—and wrote a prescription, which was filled at a drugstore. The doctor did not think the women were seriously ill; after all, it was summertime in the era before air conditioning and adequate home refrigeration. Victuals were likely to spoil on hot days, and food poisoning was as common as tapeworms, bedbugs and cholera. Dr. Brennan's medicine did not help; in fact, the patients' agony only increased, and by noon (as a reporter wrote with a barely suppressed leer) "cold sweat was standing on the bared bosom of each." They suffered from a menu of miserable symptoms, including stomach cramps, cold feet, dilated eyes and vomiting blood. It was clear by now that it was a case of poisoning.

The lovely Mrs. Sherrill was not a homeless, friendless, down-on-her-luck prostitute. She was, in fact, from a prominent local family and had been married for only a year to the eminently respectable Edward Sherrill, a traveling salesman for B.F. Avery and Sons, who did not know that his blushing bride worked part time in a whorehouse while he was away on trips. Mrs. Sherrill pathetically cried out that she wanted to be carried home so that her husband would not find out her secret shame. "Oh, for God's sake let me go!" she cried. "Take me home. I'm dying." There was no time to do so, and she was placed in the room beside Mrs. Austin's.

Dr. Brennan was recalled, along with Dr. Corrigan. They could do nothing. By the time they arrived, the women were barely alive, and their bodies were stiffening. The Man in the Glowing Nightgown came for Mrs. Sherrill at 12:45 p.m. As Mrs. Austin lay on her deathbed, she feared that her son had also been poisoned and was relieved when he came home from school. "Don't go away, for I'm going to die," she told him. Mrs. Austin entered the Void two hours after Mrs. Sherrill's demise.

The *Courier-Journal* ran drawings of the women's bodies lying peacefully in their beds under heavy covers. Considering that the location was a brothel and that it was a hot September, one suspects that the covers were a touch of artistic license added to not offend the sensibilities of readers. Both women had their jaws bound by a mortician before the newspaper artist made it to the scene, and in his illustrations they looked as if they were merely suffering from toothache.

The coroner's inquest was held at once—right there in the house. The first witness was Lloyd Austin, who told about the ice cream the inhabitants had eaten the night before. It was unlikely that the confection had been poisoned because, while Lloyd had gotten a bit sick after eating it, he had eaten more than anyone in the house, and no one else had come down with any symptoms.

The next witness was Nellie Koch, the madam's grown daughter, who lived at Tenth and Green, "having left my mother's house several weeks ago." She had visited during her mother's final illness. Mrs. Koch claimed that the dying woman told her that she and Mrs. Sherrill had become violently ill just moments after eating breakfast. Mrs. Koch had tidied up the potential crime scene by throwing away the batter that had been used to make the batter cakes.

Mrs. Johnson told of hearing the cries of the sufferers. Dr. Brennan testified that he had no idea what was the cause of death but darkly hinted that it might have been the ice cream after all: "I have known of cases where ice cream poisoning did not begin until several hours after eating."

Mrs. Sherrill. *From the* Louisville Courier-Journal *of September 11, 1892. Reprinted courtesy of the* Courier-Journal.

Mrs. Austin, post mortem. *From the* Louisville Courier-Journal *of September 10, 1892. Reprinted courtesy of the* Courier-Journal.

Laundress Rachel Jackson, professional cleaner of brothel linen, stated that her daughter had eaten the ice cream to no ill effect.

The news reports state that the coroner's inquest had to be put on hold temporarily, as "other witnesses…could not be found." They must have been referring to the young man who supposedly had paid for Mrs. Sherrill's attentions the night before the poisoning.

After the testimony, Coroner Berry autopsied Mrs. Austin; for some reason, he did not perform one on Mrs. Sherrill. He placed Mrs. Austin on a cooling board and removed her stomach. Dr. Berry could tell by looking that the victim had ingested some powerful poison such as arsenic, and he sent the gruesome relic away for a chemical analysis. He thought perhaps a then-popular pesticide called Rough on Rats had somehow fallen into the breakfast batter, but none could be found in the house, so the deaths were not accidental. Since no one in the house had died after eating ice cream the night before, the poison undoubtedly had been hidden in the breakfast.

Before they were carted away, the bodies of the two fallen women were placed side by side in a bed so that a great crowd of citizens could pass through and look at them—for no other reason, it appears, than to satisfy their curiosity. Naturally, the unnecessary spectators unintentionally destroyed potential clues at the crime scene. Many of these visitors were also prostitutes. They expressed sorrow for the women's fate, especially pretty young Mrs. Sherrill. It is difficult to judge which characters in the sordid story to feel the most sympathy for: the women who died such wretched deaths, their disgraced and motherless children or the husband of Mrs. Sherrill, who was astounded when he returned home and discovered that his newlywed bride was not only dead but also had been a lady of the evening. When he left on his last business trip, she had told him that she was going to visit her father in Tip Top, Meade County. A reporter was on hand when Mr. Sherrill saw his wife's body at Wyatt and Cralle's funeral parlor and recorded for posterity his despairing, nearly insane denial of the truth. Holding her body in his arms, Sherrill said:

> *Oh, Genie, Genie, I forgive you. I will not believe these vile stories. You were true to me. It is all false. You told me she* [presumably, he referred to Mrs. Austin] *was a nice woman, didn't you, Genie? And I never will believe it. Oh, I want to kiss you, Genie, but then I must not touch your lips, for you were poisoned, and you died in that bad house. Why don't you talk to me? Maybe you will after a while. It is not true. You are not dead.*

He continued in this vein for fifteen minutes before dumbstruck witnesses. He ended by saying, "Yes, Genie, my wife, I would love so much to kiss you, but you were poisoned." While this harrowing scene took place, Mrs. Austin's funeral was held in her own brothel. Her coffin was placed in the

Mrs. Sherrill, post mortem. *From the* Louisville Courier-Journal *of September 10, 1892. Reprinted courtesy of the* Courier-Journal.

front parlor where she died. The inmates covered all the house's mirrors with towels—an ancient superstition among practitioners of the oldest profession, but no one could say when, where or why the custom originated. One of her pallbearers was a member of the fire department with whom she had allegedly been on the most intimate of terms. Later that day, she was buried at Cave Hill Cemetery, no doubt to the embarrassment of the graveyard's proprietors. Ordinarily they would never have permitted such besmirching of sacred ground, but Mrs. Austin had purchased the plot long before her occupation became public knowledge, and there was nothing they could do about it. Mrs. Sherrill was sent home to Meade County and buried in Garnettsville. Her funeral was one of the county's most largely attended in many years. Hundreds of people visited her grave, many of whom preferred to remember her when she had still been Eugenia McCracken, before her life took a wrong turn into scandal and murder.

There were few clues to go around but plenty of theories. Nellie Koch, Mrs. Austin's daughter, thought it was a case of murder-suicide. "I have reason to believe," she said, "that mother deliberately placed poison in her breakfast, and allowed, for what reason I don't know, Mrs. Sherrill to die with her. It could not have been an accident, for mother was not in the habit of keeping poison in her kitchen. And then there would have been a box, a paper or some of the poison left in the kitchen if it had been accidental. But none of these was found." Coroner Berry agreed with her, as did Mrs. N. Johnson of Cincinnati, who only two weeks earlier had joined Mrs. Austin's house. Mrs. Johnson was the first person on the scene when the two women entered their death agonies, and she related that while Mrs. Sherrill clung piteously to life and begged to see a doctor, Mrs. Austin did not seem to care whether she lived or died, although she did complain about the incredible pain she was in.

Mrs. Austin's funeral, held in her house of ill repute. *From the* Louisville Courier-Journal *of September 11, 1892. Reprinted courtesy of the* Courier-Journal.

Mrs. Austin's brother, Sam Gore, was serving a ten-year sentence for murder in the penitentiary at Jeffersonville, Indiana; she had visited him recently, and a guard overheard her saying that she "would end her trouble." In addition, the newspapers pointed out that Mrs. Austin had recently insured herself, making her son, Lloyd, the beneficiary, and that she had shooed him off to school that morning even though he was not feeling well, before he could eat breakfast.

Mrs. Koch did not say why she thought her mother had committed suicide, but a reporter discovered that the two had recently had a falling out, during the course of which Mrs. Austin had asked her daughter to live a better life—to which Mrs. Koch replied something to the effect of, "*Well!* You're a fine one to talk!" and moved into a different house. But why would Mrs. Austin choose to dispatch herself in such a torturous manner? And why would she have taken poor Mrs. Sherrill with her?

Another rather obvious theory was that the women had been poisoned by a customer who did not want his association with them known. The aforementioned Mrs. N. Johnson said there had been at least four or five men in Mrs. Austin's house on the night before the poisonings. (The evening's festivities had begun with young Mrs. Sherrill playing—darkest of ironies!—"Nearer My God to Thee" on the piano, which seems a tune more appropriate for annihilating lust than inciting it.) Two of the visitors had stayed overnight; either or both could have slipped an unwanted surprise ingredient in the breakfast before leaving. Mrs. Johnson remembered that one of them had been called Will. Nellie Koch, who was furious with Mrs. Johnson for revealing the house's secrets, nevertheless provided another clue when she claimed that an unnamed "well-known young Main Street clerk" had visited her mother on the night in question. This news, when published, surely gave uncomfortable moments to many a Main Street clerk. A number of unsuspected men voluntarily came to newspaper offices and police stations in order to deny having had anything to do with the poisonings. The net effect, of course, was that they might as well have admitted that they had consorted with prostitutes.

Coroner Berry's inquest continued on September 12. It accomplished little, but on the same day he received an anonymous letter written in a painstaking manner that made it obvious that the author had attempted to disguise his/her penmanship. I reproduce it exactly as written in all its eccentric glory:

Dr. Berry: That Poison Was intended For Vince Spaninger And Mrs. Austin. He Ate His Meals Thair, And He Has Bin Keeping A Woman for Twenty years. She Lives at 117 West Walnut, And Tha All Had A Fight And it Has not A more than. And she said she would Kill Him if She Caught Him in The Austin House. Enclosed You will find some of The Drug That Was used. Now find out who used it, Spaninger's Wife or Mrs. Cole or Nelly Koch. Nelly and Her mother had the fuss about Him. The only Regret is that the Poisoning of The Innocent One. It is No secret About the way Spaninger And the Austin woman lived. All Second street know it. Policeman Sweeney Can Tell you if you Want to Know if He will talk.

Anney Myers,
Betty Harper,
John Snyder,
Jake Dehl.
It is to be hoped you will Find the Guilty one.

Vince Spaninger was a well-known and very married produce merchant. It will be remembered that Mrs. Austin's establishment was located above his shop, and it appears that he found it convenient to have a bordello located so close by. To sum up the unknown author's contentions: Somebody had intended to poison Mrs. Austin and her regular customer Vince Spaninger but had inadvertently poisoned Mrs. Sherrill in his place. Spaninger was the reason Mrs. Austin had recently quarreled with her daughter, Nellie Koch, and the letter implied that Spaninger's unnamed mistress had committed the poisonings. True to his/her word, the writer had included a white powder that the police immediately sent for testing. If it did turn out to be poison—and if it had been used in the commission of the murders—how had the letter writer gotten hold of it?

The same writer who had mailed the anonymous note to the coroner had made the last decade of Spaninger's life a misery by intermittently sending letters to his wife, Lizzie, informing her in lurid detail about her husband's clandestine doings. He had always indignantly denied it, but his denying days were over when some of the specifics mentioned in the note were corroborated. Spaninger admitted that he was a longtime patron of brothels. The police officer mentioned in the letter—whose name was Frank Feeny, not Sweeney—unmasked Spaninger as one of the men who had stayed overnight at Mrs. Austin's, making it plausible that he had been either the poisoner or one of the villain's intended victims. It had been his idea for Mrs. Austin to make batter cakes for breakfast, but he hurried off to his produce market before the meal was served.

The author of the letter had claimed that Spaninger's side girlfriend—one of many—lived at 117 West Walnut Street. The police and enterprising reporters went there and found Josephine Cole, age forty, who claimed to be descended from British royalty and made side money by charging fifty cents for psychic readings. She apparently was a minor-league madam, but she claimed that she merely let rooms to young ladies and had no control over what her renters chose to do. When told that she had been implicated in the letter, Mrs. Cole had no qualms about admitting something most women would have found mortifying, particularly in 1892. She said that she had been Spaninger's mistress for the last fifteen years and had tried to prevent him from marrying his wife, Lizzie. She also said that she had been jealous of Spaninger's relations with Mrs. Austin—he was such a good catch, after all!—but denied having done anything to harm her streetwalking rival. She confirmed the letter's claim that Spaninger had been the topic of the argument between Mrs. Austin and Nellie Koch. She claimed to have no insight, however, into the authorship of the letter that had exposed her affair to the world, remarking in what seems an oddly jocular tone, "Well, I'll declare! I'll bet it is the same person that sent so many to Mrs. Spaninger. And the funny thing is the letters were all true—every word of them." Mrs. Cole added to the mystery by stating that whoever sent those malevolent missives seemed to know her every action:

> *I don't see how the person found the things out, but everything that Mr. Spaninger did was reported to his wife. Why, I made him a present of a pair of slippers once for a Christmas gift, and before I gave them to him the facts were reported to his wife. For another Christmas present I painted him a picture. He took it out home with him, and do you know that almost before he had hung it up, Mrs. Spaninger got an anonymous letter about the present.*

On another occasion, the letter writer told the long-suffering Mrs. Spaninger about her husband's plan to hire a young redhead to clean their house while she visited relatives in Illinois. He must have had more than spotless furniture on his mind, or at least his wife suspected he did, because she put a stop to it. The writer also dropped dark hints that her husband had sired a boy named Ben by some unknown woman, which rumor appears to have been true; at any rate, Spaninger did not deny it. He led quite an exciting life for a seller of produce, and the righteous citizens of Louisville probably never looked at their vegetables in quite the same way again.

If Mrs. Spaninger had any illusions about her husband's fidelity, those dreams were cruelly shattered in newspaper headlines over the next several days. Judging from the illustrations in the papers, Spaninger was a reputable-looking fellow with a moustache roughly the size of a crow, as was the fashion of the time. He stated that his wife had started getting those anonymous letters shortly before they were married and that she never believed anything in them and eventually started throwing them away without reading them. He thought he knew who wrote them but had no solid proof. The claims made in the latest communication were all lies as usual, he said, and he did not believe Mrs. Austin had committed suicide.

Next to be interviewed was Nellie Koch. She denied having had the reported argument with her mother, adding, "The person that sent that letter must have committed the deed, else how could she have got hold of the poison? I think when they catch the letter writer they will have the guilty party."

The letter author's purpose in listing the four names at the end was unknown, but it was assumed they were people who could vouch for the story. They were summoned to appear at the coroner's inquest but turned out to be little help. Betty Harper, a former prostitute, had not known Mrs. Austin and had not kept in touch with her former toilers since "retiring from the business." Annie Myers pled ignorance, as did John Snyder and Jacob Diehl, Spaninger's current and former business partners, respectively; both claimed not to know that a house of prostitution was located over their store. Diehl added the potentially useful information that he had overheard Spaninger say he thought Josephine Cole was the anonymous writer who caused him so much trouble. Had Mrs. Cole been attempting to draw suspicion away from herself by pretending not to know the author's identity?

Dr. Kastenbine tested the white powder that had been sent in the mail and found that it was arsenic. The poison was easily procured in 1892—it could have been extracted from any number of pesticides, herbicides or even patent

Vince Spaninger. *From the* Louisville Courier-Journal *of September 15, 1892. Reprinted courtesy of the* Courier-Journal.

medicines—so it was possible that the author of the anonymous note had gotten it in some innocuous manner. If the analysis of Mrs. Austin's stomach proved she had been poisoned with arsenic, the white powder would be evidence worth considering. However, the wheels of justice ground to an ignominious halt when the state had difficulty getting Mrs. Austin's stomach tested. Dr. Kastenbine asked a $300 fee, which the state found too exorbitant to consider. Hard as it is to believe, at the time Kentucky had no law providing funds for expensive chemical analyses in cases of suspected poisoning, and undoubtedly many a murder went unsolved because of it. Chemist Dr. J.P. Barnum offered to do the job for $50 and got the assignment.

When Detectives Fow and Gorley visited Josephine Cole's house on September 14, Gorley noticed that the handwriting on the back of a photo of Spaninger looked like the penmanship on the anonymous letter. "Did you write this?" Gorley asked. When Cole admitted that she had, he arrested her. She broke down and confessed that she was indeed the letter writer who had tormented the vegetable baron and his wife for over a decade. She had wanted to break up the marriage so she could have the Romeo of the Radishes all to herself. Or, she explained further, she had written *some* of the letters over the years; the others were written by yet another mistress named Maggie Faulkner, whose name never figured in the case again. (Spaninger had managed to convince each of the five or so women in his life that she was the only one he truly cared about.) Not to give away the ending, but the identity of the letter writer was the only part of the mystery that was ever solved.

But if Mrs. Cole sent the anonymous letter, had the poison she included been used in the murders? She told investigators that on Friday, September 9—the morning Austin and Sherrill ate their poisoned breakfast and died in agony—she had been visited by a noticeably nervous Spaninger. Neither Austin nor Sherrill was dead at the time of his visit, but he remarked that the two women were goners for sure. When the perspiring Spaninger withdrew a handkerchief from his pocket, a brown packet wrapped in a rubber band fell out. Suspicious that it might be a love letter to some other woman—not a baseless concern—Mrs. Cole stepped forward and surreptitiously covered it with her foot. Spaninger did not notice, and when he left she opened it and realized it was poison. She did nothing until three days later, when she found out that Spaninger had been discussing more than the nutritious virtues of vegetables with Mrs. Austin. Jealousy overtook her; she was convinced that her lover was a murderer and thought it her civic duty to send Coroner Berry the white powder along with an anonymous note in which she mentioned the names of anyone she thought might help the police make a case against Spaninger—and in which she named herself as a prime suspect along with Mrs. Spaninger and Nellie Koch.

After hearing this unlikely story, detectives arrested Spaninger. Mrs. Cole claimed that Spaninger's motive for poisoning Mrs. Austin was that he preferred to while away dull care in the company of the madam's daughter, Nellie Koch. Naturally, Spaninger denied having committed murder or having had any packets of poison on his person when he visited Mrs. Cole; he furthermore claimed that Cole was the poisoner. He promised he would tell all he knew at the upcoming inquest, paid $5,000 in bail and was free.

Detectives scoured Louisville's drugstores in search of clues. At one, the clerk said a woman who resembled Mrs. Cole had bought arsenic on September 10—the morning *after* the crime, which suggests that if the purchaser were Mrs. Cole, she had been hatching a vengeful plot to drum up false charges of murder against Vince Spaninger. Unfortunately, the clerk had not kept a record of who bought the poison even though he was required by law to do so.

The big problem detectives faced in the Austin-Sherrill poisoning was not a lack of clues but rather too many of them. There were a number of plausible suspects: Mr. Spaninger, Josephine Cole, Nellie Koch and even Mrs. Austin herself. Spaninger had been in the company of Mrs. Austin the night before the poisonings and left without eating breakfast. Perhaps the women had threatened blackmail and he solved his problem by murdering them? As a businessman with a weakness for seamy extramarital affairs, he certainly had many secrets he wished to remain concealed. Josephine Cole admittedly had been jealous of every woman who had caught Spaninger's roving eye but especially of Mrs. Austin. Nellie Koch allegedly had been her own mother's rival for Spaninger's affections; as Mrs. Austin lay dying, she begged her daughter not to touch anything on the breakfast table—which indicates that her death was not a suicide—yet Nellie threw away the batter. Did she deliberately destroy evidence? Nellie had had a vicious argument with her wayward mother recently, and it was remarked that she seemed emotionless when informed of her mother's awful death. Then there were witnesses who swore that Mrs. Austin had been depressed and self-destructive lately, but why she should have taken Eugenia Sherrill to the grave with her no one could fathom. The *Courier-Journal* said the whole thing was a plot fit for Sardou, French author of plays then considered the last word in depravity.

The press titillated readers with more details about Nellie Koch's checkered past. She married her first husband, Gilbert Brockman, a brakeman for the Louisville & Nashville Railroad (L&N), in Louisville in 1886. Soon afterward, they moved to LaGrange, Oldham County, where they lived in the Russell Hotel. They were soon evicted because of her bad reputation; the Brockmans were kicked out of a couple other residences for the same reason. At one point, Mr. Brockman attempted to murder an L&N conductor, one of his wife's former admirers, at her command. In June 1887, the adventurous couple moved to Worthville, Carroll County, where Nellie kept up her hard-won reputation as a woman of low morals. A couple months later, Brockman took ill; Nellie had him shipped to a hospital in distant Cincinnati. He died three days after his arrival, and rumor held that she had poisoned him. She indignantly denied committing murder but was notably quiet about the other colorful charges. The Cincinnati doctors, when consulted, agreed that Brockman died from natural causes.

When the coroner's inquest continued on September 16, it proved a paltry letdown to persons expecting explosive revelations and invigorating scandals. They got instead inconsequential testimony from one trivial witness after another. Vince Spaninger, the lettuce-selling libertine, had been promising that he would "tell all" when he got on the stand; when the opportunity came, he had no insight into the crime except for "a theory," and he chose not to divulge even that. He told of how he had been invited to partake of the deadly breakfast and would have done so if not for pressing business. After an hour's work that morning, Emma Austin's probable employee, Mrs. N. Johnson, ran into the store and told him of the stricken women upstairs. He provided first aid and then called for the doctor, but Austin and Sherrill died despite his best efforts.

Nellie Koch's interesting testimony named some of her mother's frequent customers, including three who were overnight guests at the brothel on the night before the poisoning: William Niehoff and two firemen, William Duff and Johnnie Merten. When asked why she threw out the batter she could only say that at the time, despite the litany of horrifying symptoms, she did not realize that her mother had been poisoned.

"Did you and your mother have any trouble about Spaninger?" asked the accused man's lawyer, Aaron Kohn.

"No, not a bit," replied Nellie. "Mr. Spaninger never said a lewd word to me in my life."

Surprisingly, Josephine Cole, who thoroughly enjoyed her stay in jail—she was even allowed a visit by her poodle—was not called to appear at the inquest. On the other hand, the Annie Myers who had been mentioned in the anonymous letter was summoned but was not called to testify. The

Courier-Journal described her as "a finely-dressed, fat and very prepossessing young woman, [who] was very much annoyed over the publicity that the inquest would give her. She did not care, she said, to have her reputation compromised in any such manner." Two other witnesses were summoned but did not appear, to everyone's disappointment: former policeman James Brown and Mrs. N. Johnson, Mrs. Austin's "boarder" from Cincinnati. Both were to testify that they had seen Spaninger climbing through Mrs. Austin's window at four o'clock on the morning of the poisonings. (What had Mr. Brown and Mrs. Johnson been doing together at Austin's house at 4:00 a.m.? What you'd expect, which casts grave doubt on her claim that she thought she had been boarding in a respectable house.) Of course, Spaninger might have been sneaking around there on business, so to speak, rather than to commit murder.

As the inquest ended, Dr. Barnum announced that he had found arsenic in Mrs. Austin's stomach. The jury's verdict: the women had died of poison administered by an unknown person.

Mrs. N. Johnson—whose real name, it appears, was Lydia B. Anderson—came to Louisville on September 20 to testify before the grand jury. The authorities thought she knew more about the poisonings than anyone except the actual murderer. She had fled the city when she realized that the coroner would want her to testify, but before she left, she gave an earful to Mary Curtis and Alice Fielder, two of her "bosom friends." (That's the *Courier-Journal*'s phrase, not mine.) The newspaper got the secret information from Mrs. Johnson's confidantes and had no scruples about printing it before legal proceedings began—in fact, before even the coroner heard it.

The women functioned as Mrs. Johnson's cheering section. Mrs. Fielder told the reporter, "This Mrs. Johnson knows it all!" Said Mary Curtis, "Mrs. Johnson can tell it all." Johnson's story was that when she came downstairs on the morning of September 9 and found Mrs. Austin and Mrs. Sherrill in the agonies of poison, she asked Nellie Koch to fetch a doctor. Koch seemed strangely lackadaisical, if not reluctant, about fetching a physician for her dying mother. As already noted, the stricken Mrs. Austin had instructed Nellie not to throw out the batter, but she did anyway. Unfeelingly, Nellie and Vince Spaninger drank beer and laughed while Austin and Sherrill were in their death throes. Worst of all, when the women's lives were nearly extinct, Nellie stripped them of their jewelry.

Despite the overabundance of suspects and lack of solid evidence, the grand jury took up the matter on September 21. When Mrs. N. Johnson took the stand, her testimony was less gripping than expected. She recanted the baroque details she had told Mrs. Fielder and Mrs. Curtis. Her testimony proved nothing more than that Mrs. Koch was heartless—but not necessarily homicidal—and that Vince Spaninger liked to visit his mistress Mrs. Austin via her window rather than the staircase. Mrs. Johnson had not been alarmed at the time when she and Mr. Brown heard someone—who may or may not have been Spaninger, but let's assume it was—climbing through the window. The inference was that Austin often received gentleman callers in this unorthodox but discreet fashion. Mr. Brown was certain the prowler had been Spaninger but claimed that Mrs. Johnson had confused the date and that they had seen Spaninger making like a burglar on the morning of Wednesday, September 7, not on the morning of Friday the ninth. There was no new evidence, and there were no new witnesses; those who testified could only tell the flimsy stories they had already told. "We have a world of evidence, without one scintilla of proof," said Judge Thompson. All charges were dropped. Vince Spaninger and Josephine Cole walked away as free as the robins of spring. Mrs. Cole had had such a good time and eaten so well in jail that she seemed to regret being turned loose.

Three weeks after the poisonings, Mrs. Austin's elegant whorehouse furniture was sold at auction. Perhaps some of it still exists, to the delight of owners blissfully ignorant of its provenance. Mr. Spaninger, Mrs. Cole and Mrs. Koch returned to their normal lives—or at least, lives as normal as it is possible to lead after such a humiliating and public scrutiny of the skeletons in their closets. Rachel Jackson probably took up the washing at some other residence—a convent or a charm school this time, let us hope. Mrs. Anderson was heard from again in November of that eventful year, when the *Cincinnati Commercial Gazette* reported that she was in court testifying against her sister Anna Duncan's son-in-law, Alf Vonderheide, on a charge of beating Mrs. Duncan.

The Austin-Sherrill poisoning was never solved. On September 18, the *Courier-Journal* ran an editorial summing up the facts: "The Second Street murder mystery is one of the most atrocious and puzzling in the annals of crime. The authorities seem lost in a maze of clues, and all that is clear is that two women are dead and somebody should be hanged." Most people thought that that somebody was Josephine Cole, Nellie Koch or Vince Spaninger. There was good reason to consider each as a major suspect. Mrs. Cole admitted to writing harassing letters to Mr. and Mrs. Spaninger over the years. In the anonymous note to the coroner, Dr. Berry, she wrote: "The only regret is…the poisoning of the innocent one." Was Mrs. Cole only guessing that the murderer felt guilty about accidentally killing Mrs. Sherrill? Or did she know how the killer felt because she actually *was* the killer? On the other hand, the poison she had mailed with the letter was not conclusively tied to the crime. Likely, it was arsenic she had procured and sent to the coroner to get her faithless lover Spaninger in hot water.

Did Nellie Koch murder Mrs. Austin because she was jealous over Spaninger and/or because she resented her mother's pleadings that she "live a virtuous life"? She tidied up the crime scene after being instructed not to, thereby destroying potential evidence—intentionally or not.

Vincent Spaninger is an attractive suspect due to his proximity to the crime scene, the fact that he turned down the poisoned breakfast—perhaps providentially, perhaps not—and the fact that he had many secrets to hide and many women to hide them from. But poisoning a couple of prostitutes who kept house in the upper floor of his store would be a certain way to court, rather than avoid, bad publicity.

Or was it a murder-suicide, as many thought from the beginning? The defense argued that Mrs. Austin became jealous of Spaninger's attentions to Mrs. Sherrill and intended to poison the three of them at breakfast, but fortunately for the Carrot Casanova, he had to get to work and skipped the Most Important Meal of the Day. Evidence also pointed to Mrs. Austin. Scientists examined all the ingredients of the batter and found poison in none of them. Whoever committed the crimes must have put arsenic *in the finished batter*, which Nellie Koch had thrown out, not in one particular ingredient. Spaninger and Mrs. Austin were the only suspects known to be present when the batter was produced.

Considering that several customers had access to Mrs. Austin's establishment—including some who were there the night before the murders—perhaps the killer was never suspected. Might a client have stayed later in the house than anyone thought and poisoned the batter on his way out? At least four men other than Spaninger were known to have spent the night of September 8 in the house, yet none was called to testify. Perhaps one of them could have provided information that would have solved the mystery.

Whether Spaninger was the poisoner, it is almost certain that his fickle affections were the reason the murders occurred, a thought that could not have made him happy. Evidently, his wife, Lizzie, forgave all and stayed with her husband; they are buried side by side in Cave Hill Cemetery. He died in June 1928; she outlived him by fourteen years.

6

Your Friendly
Neighborhood Pornographer

In September 1893, R.W. McAfee, a United States Post Office inspector in
St. Louis who was in charge of the post offices of fifteen states, was notified
that obscene material was being sent through the mail. According to the
contemporary press, the material consisted of "a large number of catalogues,
the contents of which were of the vilest description. Almost every obscene
word imaginable was published in full in these catalogues." Not only that, but
somebody was sending photos of women posing in the nude!

It was McAfee's job to apprehend the scoundrel. He got one of the
catalogues and found that he had "seen nothing like it," even though he had
spent years studying obscene material sent via the hallowed U.S. mail (hey,
it was part of his job). According to the catalogue's sales pitch, a sporting
person could get sets of photos ranging in cost from $4 to $10 (the equivalent
in modern currency would be nearly $100 and $250, so the dirty pictures
were not cheap). The catalogue included the claim that it had been printed
by "the Metropolitan Art Company of New York City." However, it urged,
do not send the money directly to the Metropolitan Art Company but rather
to its manager, who was allegedly "Fred Malloy, post office box 421 or 491,
Louisville, Ky."

On October 4, Inspector McAfee came to Louisville looking for this Fred
Malloy fellow. Surveillance was conducted on post office boxes 421 and 491,
but no one collected mail from them. McAfee left the city, unable to flush
out his quarry, but he returned in November, this time bearing loads of
evidence: photos, catalogues and pornographic literature.

McAfee set a trap. He wrote a letter to Malloy requesting a set of those hot pictures. Malloy obligingly sent a catalogue. The inspector sent some money—and then, on November 17, hid in the Louisville post office. At noon, a tall, well-dressed, prosperous-looking young man opened box 421 and removed the order sent by McAfee. The postal official stepped out of hiding and had his culprit.

The peddler of porno turned out not to be named Fred Malloy but Henry Zink, a married man with several children. He was the publisher of the *Southern Wheelman*, a Louisville publication that catered to bicycle enthusiasts. Zink confessed that he had printed and mailed the catalogues and literature and also distributed the photos, but he claimed he had not personally taken the pictures. They had been snapped by a "well-known Louisville photographer," whose name the inspector at first declined to give to the press.

The *Southern Wheelman* was not a financial success, nor was a short-lived publication Zink started called *Wit and Humor*. In 1892, he had been kicked out of the Louisville Cycle Club for failure to pay his dues. His friends, who did not know Zink had become a hometown pornography baron, wondered about the source of his newfound prosperity. In his last venture, at least, Zink was successful beyond his wildest dreams. Among his best customers were saloon owners across the nation—including local ones—who had purchased entire albums of his pictures to entertain patrons of discriminating tastes.

The purchaser of porn in that era had to be careful, lest he—I assume it was almost invariably a he—be hornswoggled by unscrupulous vendors who knew their dupes were in no position to complain to the authorities. For example, at the turn of the century, a shady firm distributed circulars at saloons and other places frequented by rowdies that read, "On receipt of $1 we will send, securely sealed, a beautifully bound book of 400 pages, full of good things. Every sport should have one. The most wonderful book ever written. French and English translation. Prohibited in some countries. Write at once." Lecherous gents who sent a dollar received a fifteen-cent Bible in return. The same stunt was attempted by a Michigan man, who advertised sale of "the King of Books," which could be purchased for two dollars, cash only. However, the stuff Zink was selling appears to have been the real deal, at least by the standards of 1893. Inspector McAfee and Detective Bauer searched Zink's office and found hundreds of pictures, which the press described as "the vilest that had ever been under their observation. They will be preserved as evidence and then destroyed." Compounding the scandal, authorities in Louisville realized that some of the pictures featured local women, though "many of the photographs...were of women of bad reputation." Zink was

Henry Zink. *From the* Louisville
Courier-Journal *of March 2,
1894. Reprinted courtesy of the*
Courier-Journal.

in serious trouble. One of his friends paid his bail, and the enterprising young man took the opportunity to immediately flee for Frankfort.

Zink fled out of shame—and possibly out of fear of getting a beating—but there was little local law enforcement could do to him because Kentucky was one of the few states in 1893 that had no law against printing obscene material; in fact, two previous legislatures had refused to pass such a law. For this reason, the Louisville police force and its detectives barely lifted a finger in helping McAfee find evidence against Zink and his yet-unnamed photographer. In one instance, detectives promised to go to the post office right after Zink was arrested but failed to show up. The *Courier-Journal* complained, "As to the law on the case, whenever a law is not covered by a specific statute the common law prevails, and to this recourse might have been had."

Zink was gone from Louisville, but in the meantime the identity of his partner, the "well-known" local photographer, was released. It was Walter Elrod, who not very convincingly denied the charge:

I have never made any obscene pictures, though I can safely say that nearly every other photographer in the city has done so. Some of them have large stocks on hand. Zink came to me about four months ago and wanted some pictures. I had three or four that were given me by a friend. They were works of art and I gave them to him, more to get rid of them than anything else.

Elrod invited police to search his gallery without a warrant. Two officers did so, but the *Courier-Journal* editorially berated their methods of evidence gathering: "When the Louisville police search a photograph gallery for obscene pictures they saunter in, pick up about twenty negatives out of several hundred, saunter out again and proclaim that there is no 'case.'"

The case degenerated into a blame game. The police said they were ready to arrest the photographer Elrod if Inspector McAfee gave them proof he was guilty. McAfee said that he could not do so unless two unnamed "reputable citizens" who claimed to have seen pornographic negatives in Elrod's studio stepped forth and swore out a warrant. McAfee finally left town without revealing the names of these citizens. One of them may have been Joseph Hutti, a photographer who told the *Courier-Journal* that he used to work for Elrod but had quit his job in a fit of moral indignation in August 1893 because his employer printed dirty pictures for customers—including a judge, who wanted forty-five dollars' worth. The disgruntled former employee claimed that Elrod had hundreds of such negatives, some of which he bought from other distributors, some of which he made himself using local women as subjects. Hutti also said he was willing to swear in court to the truth of his statements. If his story was true, it seems inconceivable that the police who searched Elrod's studio could have missed all those pictures unless they weren't looking very diligently. (Or, possibly, Elrod destroyed them as soon as he heard that his partner Zink had been caught. Hutti pointed out that the negatives were so small, a couple hundred of them could be hidden in one's pockets.)

And yet, for all his burning desire to see justice done, it seems Joseph Hutti didn't swear out a warrant against Elrod.

It seems that all this fuss and bother was being enacted to keep the public and press happy, since Kentucky had no laws against manufacturing and distributing pornography in the first place. The police's lack of interest was unmistakable, but they could hardly be faulted for lacking zeal in pursuing a case that could not be successfully prosecuted in local courts. On November 26, the *Courier-Journal* ran a column publishing the opinions of a number of prominent citizens, all of whom harrumphed that a law against obscene material should be passed, and the sooner the better. (One hyperbolic district attorney said he would rather his family be exposed to "a man in the worst stages of smallpox" than a pornographer.) In December, Senator-elect J.H. Weller promised to introduce "a drastic measure against the circulation of obscene pictures or literary matter" in the next session of the state legislature.

Henry Zink returned to Louisville on November 22. He could not be prosecuted under Kentucky law, but since he had used the U.S. mail to distribute pornography, he could still be tried under federal law. On February 28, 1894, he pled guilty to seven counts in the indictment returned by the federal grand jury and begged for the court's mercy. The photos and literature were deemed too obscene to be used as evidence, but numerous witnesses testified to Zink's "general good character" and explained that he went into the pornography racket out of desperation because his other business ventures had failed and he had a large family to support.

Judge Barr of the United States District Court asked Zink if he had anything to say on his behalf before sentence was passed. The ashen-faced man replied in words that made him seem not quite the loathsome, immoral monster the press had depicted:

> *Until last May I was getting along well in my business as a publisher. Then business got dull, and after this my stock was destroyed in the Power-building fire. I had no insurance. My father-in-law helped me to start again, but I could do nothing. My trade kept falling off until my business did not amount to anything. A local photographer induced me to handle those pictures for him. This was last August. I did not know that there was any law against selling those pictures. I am very sorry that I dealt in them. I beg you, Judge, to have mercy on me. I am a poor man. I have a nice family, and I never was in court before in my life.*

The judge replied:

> *I looked at those horrid pictures last night. I am compelled to say that you have been guilty of a very serious offense. It is a singular thing that a man who has had a mother and who has a good wife and family would deal in such terrible things as those pictures. They are the filthiest things I have ever seen, horrible, almost beyond what I thought a man could dream of. You have respectable, honest relatives. All are good people from what I can learn, but I have investigated your former character and do not find it as good as it might be.*

So saying, Judge Barr fined Zink only five dollars—but also sentenced him to two years at hard labor in the penitentiary at Jeffersonville, Indiana. "It is the general opinion that Zink got what he fully deserved," remarked the *Courier-Journal*. Those must have been *some pictures*.

There was a heart-wrenching scene when Zink arrived at the prison on March 5 and said his final goodbyes to his wife and parents. Only days after his arrival, the prisoner pleaded that his sentence be reduced on the grounds that he had tuberculosis in both lungs and had less than two years to live anyway.

But what of Walter Elrod, the photographer who furnished Zink with the licentious photos? His case was the first to be taken up by the March 1894 grand jury. Luckily for Elrod, he faced local courts rather than federal courts since, unlike Zink, he did not personally distribute material by mail and thus broke no federal laws. Elrod went to court on March 7 and pleaded not guilty. His trial date was set for April 9 and then moved to December. But what happened to him after that, I cannot say.

On December 6, 1894, Zink was pardoned by President Grover Cleveland on the basis of a statement by the prisoner's family doctor, Dr. Stanislaus Brzozowski, that he was in fact dying of tuberculosis. The physician said he had treated Zink for the disease long before his brush with the law. Poor Mrs. Zink was so overcome with joy when she got the news—about her husband's pardon, not his tuberculosis—that she immediately took sick herself and had to be confined to her bedroom. Henry Zink came home a free man on December 9.

The repentant pornographer was destined to instigate a final controversy. He was heard to joke among friends that he didn't *really* have TB, and lawmen assumed that he had pulled a fast one on prison officials and the president of the United States. Dr. David Peyton, the jail physician, confirmed that his patient was consumptive. Dr. C.W. Kelly, who had signed a petition requesting Zink's pardon, said he had treated the prisoner for tuberculosis as far back as 1891. (If Zink knew before 1893 that he was slowly dying of TB, it may explain why he seemed desperate to support his family by any means possible.)

On the other hand, according to the *Courier-Journal*, "Those who knew Zink before he was sentenced say he is healthier looking now than he was then." In addition, Dr. Brzozowski admitted that Zink was in no immediate danger of dying and could have lived another ten or fifteen years in prison, provided the jail officials did not make him work at hard labor. President Cleveland caught wind of the fact that Zink might have been faking and ordered an investigation, vowing that if the rumor turned out to be true, he would revoke the pardon and send Zink right back to prison. Cleveland took the matter so seriously that he *personally* wrote a letter to Warden J.B. Patten of the Jeffersonville Prison—he even wrote the address on the envelope rather than let a secretary do it. Evidently, Cleveland did not relish being made a fool. Warden Patten wrote back, reassuring the chief executive that the best medical opinion was that Zink was truly fatally ill.

Just to be certain, at Dr. Peyton's request Zink was examined on December 27 by professors from every medical college in Louisville. For perhaps the first and only time in the history of the world, all the medical experts agreed: the patient was doomed to die of consumption. He would last slightly less than another year and a half. On April Fools' Day 1896, thirty-three-year-old Henry Zink embarked for phantom shores.

Dr. Brzozowski was glad to have saved face. "The death of Zink by consumption was peculiarly gratifying to his physician, who felt that he was in a bad light before the public," remarked the *Courier-Journal's* obituary.

7

What Came of a Marriage between a Murderer and a Prostitute

Being from a "fine old family" has its advantages if one does not waste them. Take Mr. and Mrs. Albert Wing, for example. Both came from good stock and should have made something of themselves—something other than a murderer and a corpse, respectively.

Albert E. (Bert) Wing was the son of Samuel Wing, who had been one of the most prominent merchants of Owensboro, Daviess County, until the Civil War bankrupted him. Albert's elder brother, Ramsey, was the United States minister to Ecuador during President Grant's administration. All of the Wing children were said to be highly intelligent, well educated and given every opportunity to shine. (For all that, it appears that murderous blood ran through the veins of the family's males. Bert's brother Charles spent ten years in jail for killing the marshal of Princeton, Caldwell County; another brother, Samuel Jr., decided to kill himself in Salt Lake City in March 1908. His suicide was notable for the meticulous care he took in planning every detail, including paying a barber in advance for a shave "good enough for a wedding or a funeral.") In 1892, Bert Wing, at age thirty-five, was tall and slender, sandy haired and mustached. He was quiet by nature, but his quietness masked a mean streak that came to the forefront when he drank, which appears to have been the majority of the time.

Wing's wife was Miriam G. Eaves, daughter of Judge Charles Eaves of Greenville, Muhlenberg County; her nickname was "Kitty." Like her husband, Kitty was born into a wealthy, privileged family. Unfortunately, she had a habit of letting her biological urges dictate her behavior, and she had a reputation for precocious wildness. She married Edward Reno of Greenville when she was fifteen years old, but after having two children by him, she decided that marriage was not to her liking. Prostitution seemed an ideal vocation to her, so she ran away and joined a brothel in St. Louis. And later, another one in Memphis, Tennessee. And another one in Evansville, Indiana.

In 1882, while she was working in the St. Louis bordello, she took up with fellow Kentuckian Bert Wing. Despite the fact that she was still officially Mrs. Reno, she moved in with him. Wing was consumed with jealousy—perhaps he should have thought twice about having a prostitute for a girlfriend—and around 1885, he shot to death one of her regulars, Joseph Glenn, a shoe company clerk formerly from Owensboro. Wing was given ten years of hard labor in the penitentiary.

Kitty, seemingly contrite, was placed by her father in a St. Louis convent. After a year, she moved back to Greenville, but her reformation was temporary; before long, she was again ensconced in a St. Louis brothel under the false name Essie Davis. A couple years later, she made another attempt at changing her life: she entered a second convent in Wisconsin, where she was an accomplished music teacher.

In the spring of 1890, Missouri's Governor Francis pardoned Bert Wing after he had served only four years of his sentence. Wing moved to Greenville, where he worked for a tobacco company. Kitty came to Greenville one day to visit her poor, disgraced father, bumped into her old flame Wing and immediately stepped off the straight and narrow path. On May 1, 1891, the two were married in Muhlenberg County over her father's strenuous objections. They seemed to get along well until Kitty reverted to her accustomed ways, left Bert and moved to Louisville in December. He followed her a couple of weeks later.

By all accounts, Mrs. Wing was easy on the eyes. She was four years younger than her husband and had blue eyes and jet black hair; she was quiet and ladylike—or seemed to be, anyway—well educated, a good conversationalist and a talented pianist. Her big secret, and it really wasn't much of a secret, was that as soon as she moved to Louisville she commenced working at Myrtle (Merty) Edwards's brothel at 730 West Green Street. It is doubtful that Kitty's clients were much interested in her superior education, conversational powers and musical ability.

The working girls at Merty's probably provocatively smoked cigarettes in front of customers, showed off their bare ankles, flounced immodestly about with only four petticoats on, gave coquettish looks—they may even have winked!—or whatever it is that wicked women did to entice men in that bygone era. There was a consensus among the laborers at Merty's: they all liked Kitty Wing but loathed her sullen, temperamental husband, who was decidedly not happy to find that his beloved had taken up business at the old stand. Kitty told her co-worker Lillie Roberts that she was sure Bert would kill her someday. Yet she would not stay away from him. She explained that she was in love with Wing, and "she did not believe that a woman could love but once."

On September 12, 1892, witnesses saw the Wings riding in a coupe on Cane Run Road, both the worse for drink. They had an argument, the culmination of which was Wing's attempt to stab his wife. The coupe driver hurried away to find a policeman, but when the officer arrived, he found that Mr. Wing had been too intoxicated to carry out his murderous intention. It had not been through a lack of effort, however, and he had managed to give his wife a decent beating. The Wings were arrested for disorderly conduct and set loose to fulfill their destinies after they dried out.

By the night of November 1, 1892, Wing had had enough. He went with his beautiful wife to her place of business, Myrtle Edwards's brothel. They checked into an upstairs room, seemingly in the best of spirits. The inmates of the house, who, we learn from the inquest report, were enjoying "ribald music" played on the parlor piano, had their lewd polkas and bawdy waltzes disrupted by the sounds of a struggle, then a crash, then groans and then silence. Apparently, they were used to such sound effects in their place of business because no one investigated. But after a few minutes came noises they could not ignore: louder groaning, as of someone in pain. The assembled bordello employees broke down the door and found Kitty Wing lying on the floor in a bloody heap. The reader will recall that the murders of Emma Austin and Eugenia Sherrill had occurred a couple of months earlier; clearly, 1892 was a tough year for Louisville prostitutes.

The generally staid *Courier-Journal* covered the scandalous story with prose so purple that it would have been the envy of a Hearst newspaper in those days or a supermarket tabloid in ours. Its reporter described Kitty's demolished condition in lavish detail:

> *Her head was raised a few inches from the floor by means of her dark brown hair; one hand was clasped over her heart, between the fingers of which slowly flowed her life blood in tiny red streams. The bosom of her dress was covered with the crimson tide. Her head rested in a pool of blood, which crept slowly toward the door where stood with blanched faces the dying woman's sisters in sin.*

Blood had spattered every object in the room, from playing cards to the bed, which, the reporter made certain to note, was in a rumpled condition. The "sisters in sin" lifted the dying woman onto the rumpled bed and sent for a doctor. Kitty, who had been stabbed just below the heart, in the neck, in the lungs and in the back, bled out before help could arrive. But Bert Wing was nowhere to be seen: he had slipped through a window and nearly got arrested by a suspicious policeman as he walked away in as nonchalant a manner as he could muster.

Among the dead woman's effects were letters from priests and nuns beseeching her to conquer her passions and live virtuously. Investigators found a scrapbook containing clippings about Wing's murder of Joseph Glenn in St. Louis and photos of the Jefferson City prison where he had been incarcerated. From this, we may deduce that despite her many failings, Kitty at least was sentimental. The *Courier-Journal* printed an illustration showing Mrs. Wing—"beautiful even in death"—lying shrouded in the coroner's "dead room," soon to be removed by her long-suffering father for burial in Muhlenberg County, where she had spent innocent days (but not very many of them, it would appear) long ago.

The police thought Wing could not have gotten far since he was penniless when he abandoned the scene of his bloody crime, but day after day passed without a trace of him. Naturally, nervous citizens thought they saw him everywhere in the city. One man was sure that he saw Wing with his hair dyed black; another saw him in a red wig; a third thought he saw Wing wearing gold spectacles and a sombrero, a disguise that certainly would have failed to attract attention. A woman saw him "disguised as an actor," whatever that could have meant, and a pack of small boys claimed Wing was hiding out in a brewery, which at least has the ring of truth to it. Wing was spotted in hotels, theaters and restaurants, riding in public conveyances and walking the streets as though he were the mayor. The helpful witnesses were all mistaken. Wing actually had been hiding in New Orleans, where he was arrested while playing pool in a saloon on November 10. Likely, he had stopped there on the way to Mexico. He maintained later that he had been betrayed by a friend.

Within an hour of Wing's arrival and incarceration in Louisville, the jail was visited by at least one thousand people who wanted to see the man who had committed the most notorious murder the city had seen in years. He was arraigned in court on November 16 and pleaded not guilty; afterward, Wing pathetically attempted to sell his overcoat in order to raise money to pay a lawyer. Fortunately for him, his cousin H.J. Patterson, a teacher at Lexington's

Kitty Wing in the dead room. *From the* Louisville Courier-Journal *of November 3, 1892. Reprinted courtesy of the* Courier-Journal.

State University—now known as the University of Kentucky—stepped in and offered financial assistance.

Patterson might as well have not bothered. By the time Wing went to trial, he had completely lost all interest in living. He admitted his crime, changed his plea to guilty, ignored the advice of his attorneys and said that he earnestly desired to be hanged. The only thing he would not do was explain his motive for murdering his wife. It seemed manifest that Wing would get the death penalty; the prisoner himself was confident of it. But before the jury retired to determine a verdict, an elderly man stepped forward and asked to speak to the court. He was none other than Judge Eaves, father of the victim. "Your Honor," he said, "I am here to ask a favor. This man killed my daughter. He was her husband and she my daughter, and while I deplore the tragedy, I want to ask you and the jury to be merciful. This man has committed a most brutal murder, but I am an old man. My hair is white, and I will soon be ready for the grave. I want to ask that no more blood be shed. I want you to send this man, Bert Wing, to the penitentiary for life. I think this will be sufficient punishment, and I am a judge."

The impromptu speech saved Wing's neck. The jury sentenced him to life in the penitentiary at Frankfort. He began paying his debt to society on May 7, 1893.

Fifteen very slow years passed. Sentimental souls in Louisville, Greenville and Owensboro signed petitions requesting that Wing be freed, and three different wardens recommended the same. Wing himself came to think it was a great idea. Yet, to his annoyance, the parole board thought turning him loose in society might have a downside. Wing seemed a model prisoner and eventually became a trusty, gaining special privileges: he was permitted to use the outer office and got to wear a gray, unstriped uniform. He gave the prison officials reason to rethink their generosity when he escaped with another trusty, John Clark, on the afternoon of January 6, 1908. This was how Wing justified the generosity of his victim's father, whose speech to the jury had spared his life. It was suspected that a former convict, E.P. Ashcraft of Estill County, had helped Wing escape, since Ashcraft had been noticed loitering around the prison gates that day.

John Beeler of Frankfort was beaten and robbed of his clothes by two strangers shortly after the escape, and it was assumed that escapees Wing and Clark were the culprits. On January 11, Clark was arrested while playing pool in a Lexington saloon—by strange coincidence, the very activity Wing had been performing when he had been arrested for murdering Kitty—but despite a search that covered every city and town within a hundred-mile radius of Frankfort, Bert Wing eluded his pursuers.

He only eluded them until April 29, 1914, that is, when "John Thornton" confessed to the Cincinnati police that he was in fact Albert Wing. A Frankfort deputy warden traveled to Cincinnati and quickly confirmed the man's statement. Wing revealed that he had spent his years on the lam supporting himself by means of robbery in such Ohio cities as Cleveland, Galion, Crestline, Toledo and Dayton. Furthermore, he made the astounding claim that the officials at the Kentucky State Penitentiary allowed trusties to carry keys to the front gate and that they were allowed to slip away at night for a while—as long as they promised to be *really good* and come back in a few hours! Wing gave an interview to the *Frankfort State Journal* in which he described his miserable six years of freedom, when he had trusted no friend, looked over his shoulder constantly and accepted demeaning jobs since he did not dare ask anyone he knew for a reference.

Wing was taken back to Frankfort on April 30 in order to serve the rest of his life term. In his life he had been shown clemency by the governor of Missouri, who set him free to murder someone else; by the father of his victim; and by the Commonwealth of Kentucky. In 1916, the Board of Prison Commissioners decided to show him clemency once more. He was pardoned on February 11 and given a home by former warden George Chinn. If he got into any more trouble during the remainder of his life, it does not appear in the historical record.

8

Louisville's Bonnie and Clyde

D uring the Great Depression, Bonnie Parker and Clyde Barrow shared a passion for robbery and each other that made them American criminal superstars. Arthur Penn's groundbreaking and stylistically violent—but erroneous—1967 film biography has ingrained details of their lives and career in the national consciousness. (Paul Schneider's 2009 book *Bonnie and Clyde: The Lives Behind the Legends* is much more accurate than the famous film and just as tragic.)

Slightly more than a generation before Parker and Barrow shot their way across the Midwest into the realm of legend, Louisville had its own set of felonious lovers. Mattie and Howard were never as notorious as Bonnie and Clyde, but there are remarkable parallels between their stories.

In 1897, the *New York Times* began using the slogan "All the News That's Fit to Print," Sherlock Holmes was a literary sensation, Brooklyn was officially incorporated into New York City, *The Katzenjammer Kids* was one of America's first comic strips, *Cyrano de Bergerac* had its stage premiere, the world's first car dealership opened in London and Thomas Edison patented his movie camera. In Louisville, Mattie Belle Mahoney was only sixteen years old and "exceptionally pretty," according to contemporary accounts; newspaper illustrations suggest otherwise, but standards of beauty change with time. (Her first name may have been Maymie. The papers never could agree on this seemingly elementary detail.) She roomed at the Morton Home for Orphans, although her mother, Annie, was alive and dwelling at 313 Eighteenth Street. Nothing written in Mattie's own words survives, but the indications are that she—like Bonnie Parker in Dallas in 1930—was restless, bored and craving excitement and romance. Like Parker, Mattie was not overly particular about where she found it, and she appears to have been attracted to antisocial types.

Darkly handsome, mustachioed Howard Clark had a good education, but he found being a career criminal more fulfilling than his job as a clerk at the Adams Express Company. He became so adept at crime that he kept the Recording Angel as busy as possible. In 1890, he stole two packages of jewelry from his employers. He escaped conviction. In 1893, he was arrested for robbing a saloon of cigars and liquor, but his respectable relatives kept him from serving time. In 1895, he was caught burglarizing a house in Bowling Green. Again, his well-intentioned kin used their influence to keep Clark on the streets. (Ironically, we can see with hindsight that Clark would probably have lived longer and possibly gotten into less trouble if they had allowed him to take his lumps.) Afterward, he was arrested on various charges in Covington and Cincinnati.

Clark worked as a house painter when he wasn't employed in his chief occupations: safecracking and housebreaking, at which he was so skilled that it was said he had "driven the whole police force of Louisville to drink." During one of the brief periods in which he tried to make an honest living, Clark was hired to paint the orphanage where Mattie lived. He developed an infatuation with her, and she gladly returned the sentiments. Clark told Mattie that her devotion was essential to his complete happiness and implored her to become his wife; he already had a wife and a child, but in the heat of passion lovers often overlook such minor details. He inveigled Mattie to leave the Morton Home and live with him. Offended newspapers spared no ink in calling Clark a "villain" and describing his sweetheart as "innocent" and a "victim." However, this reveals more about the era's morality than it does about the facts in the case. Mattie was only too willing to be led astray.

For several months, Mattie and Howard lived together with all the side privileges that married couples enjoy. At some point they had a falling out, and Mattie, "a ruined woman," moved back in with her mother. Howard, full of sin and conceit, applied his brainpower to luring her from home again. On October 3, his associate Joe Staebler visited the Mahoney residence and, calling himself "Mr. Harry Cleaver, a wealthy stock dealer," told Mattie's mother that he wanted to hire her daughter to be a companion to his wife. Poor Mrs. Mahoney fell for it, and in short order, Mattie was back in Howard Clark's arms.

Howard Clark. *From the* Louisville Courier-Journal *of August 20, 1898. Reprinted courtesy of the* Courier-Journal.

On November 22, police in Indianapolis arrested the lovers on the lam. The girl's mother swore out a warrant against Clark on a charge of abduction. They were returned to Louisville in the company of a detective on November 25. No doubt it came as a surprise to Mattie's mother when her daughter, far from being grateful for her deliverance from Clark's wicked clutches, instead defended her alleged "enticer" and "captor." Clark was sent to jail, and Mattie was detained for disorderly conduct.

Howard Clark told a reporter that he had not seduced Mattie; heavens, no! Rather, when he first became acquainted with her at the orphanage she had complained that her mother abused her, so by running away with her he had chivalrously saved her from a *living hell*. He sanctimoniously claimed to have been so worried that one of her acquaintances, "a woman of bad reputation," might lead her astray that he had been in the act of returning her to her mother when he was arrested. (I wish the reporter had asked why, if Mattie's mother had maltreated her as Clark claimed, he had thought it in the girl's best interests to send her back home.) Despite the well-established fact that the two had lived together for several months, Clark insisted that he had treated his girlfriend "like a daughter." Considering that one of the charges against him was seduction, he might have selected a less nauseating choice of words.

After Clark palmed off this hogshead of malarkey to the journalist, Mattie wrapped her arms around Clark's neck—undoubtedly, her mother wished she could wrap her hands around the same—and said, "Mr. Clark is the best friend I ever had. He neither seduced nor abducted me. A man connected with me by marriage seduced me when I was but twelve years old. My mother never treated me right, and I was anxious to leave home. I love Mr. Clark, and will stick by him through thick and thin."

Mattie was in love with Howard, and it is possible that he loved her too. But one may be in love and still be a pervert. Clark had been overheard to boast that he had a fake marriage certificate bearing his name and Mattie's in case anyone questioned the nature of their association, and Clark exploded in anger when the reporter asked a logical question: if his relationship with Mattie was aboveboard and legal, why had he sent his stooge Joe Staebler under a bogus name to sneak the girl out of her mother's house? In short, all of Mattie's statements in the above quotation were dubious—all but the last one, which would be proved in spades a year later.

Miss Mahoney was released from jail since she really hadn't done anything illegal, but Howard Clark remained. She visited him every day. But on December 9, trouble entered paradise. Mattie told Howard that she was going to leave her mother's home again, this time without him. Clark was convinced one of the jail's turnkeys had stolen her affections. "I'll shoot him if he takes her away from me! I'll kill him if I am allowed to live," vowed Clark. On what evidence did he base this belief? Well, he had noticed the jail official in question talking to her the last time she visited—plus, he had had a dream in which Mattie and the turnkey got married, so that clinched it. It did not soothe Clark's agitated feelings when one of his so-called friends related a rumor that Mattie had gotten married in Jeffersonville. Mattie's mother swore that her difficult daughter was still

Mattie Mahoney. *From the* Louisville Courier-Journal *of October 10, 1898. Reprinted courtesy of the* Courier-Journal.

living at home and seemed satisfied with her lot in life. Mrs. Mahoney was right—half right, anyway. Mattie had not gotten married, but she was far from content with life at home.

At some undetermined point, Howard Clark was released from jail. He drops from the gimlet eyes of History until August 12, 1898, the day the Spanish-American War ended. Two Louisville policemen, Corporal Louis Whitman and Patrolman Joseph Heffernan, saw burglars trying to break into Eberle's grocery store on Twenty-first Street. One of them was Howard Clark, who drew a revolver and fired at Whitman, barely missing him. Heffernan struck Clark in the head with a nightstick; Whitman shot the second burglar in the arm. The wounded man fled. In the meantime, Clark recovered his senses enough to shoot Heffernan through the liver. Heffernan, seriously wounded, was taken to the hospital. Clark escaped in the confusion. "Unless we catch him off his guard," declared Police Chief Haager, "there will be shooting, and the officers will have to take desperate chances."

Shooting a cop was as unwise a move in 1898 as it is today, and the entire police forces of Louisville, Jeffersonville and New Albany were on the lookout for Clark and his accomplice—the latter, George Carter, was apprehended within hours. Like his latter-day counterpart and fellow cop killer Clyde Barrow, Howard Clark had a reputation for being a hard man to catch, and the authorities knew it might take a long time to find him. They almost caught him on the morning of August 13, when they staked out the Chestnut Street boardinghouse where Mattie Mahoney was now living, believing—correctly, it turned out—that he would be unable to stay away from her. The police officers must not have disguised themselves very well because Mattie spotted them and alerted her paramour, who made his escape by leaping through a rear window.

Police anger intensified on August 14, when forty-year-old Heffernan died of his wounds. He left behind a wife and two children. It probably was small comfort to the widow, but at least she collected $2,000 worth of her husband's insurance—$50,000 in modern currency—from the Improved Order of the Heptasophs, one of many long-vanished nineteenth-century fraternal orders.

Clues about Clark's whereabouts dribbled in. David Cotner, a Louisville barber, said he gave the fugitive a shave early on the morning of Sunday, August 15, three days after the shooting. "I have to catch a train," Clark had told him, "and I want you to do the job in a hurry." Cotner—who was a former policeman—noticed that his customer was in a rush, seemed inexplicably nervous and held a .44-caliber revolver in each hand while being shaved. And yet, the barber apparently saw nothing suspicious, which may explain why he was a *former* policeman. At least Cotner's close encounter proved that Clark had not left the city as of Sunday morning. The murderer's trunk was found in a room near Brook and Main Streets; it contained many stolen goods and, oddly, several dresses. But it did not yield clues revealing Clark's current location.

On the night of August 15, two burglars tried to break into John Gruber's grocery store on the corner of Twenty-eighth and St. Xavier Streets. By coincidence, Gruber was the murdered policeman's brother-in-law. An armed neighbor took potshots at the would-be thieves, who fled into the night. One was recognized as being an acquaintance of

Officer Heffernan. *From the* Louisville Courier-Journal *of August 13, 1898. Reprinted courtesy of the* Courier-Journal.

Howard Clark and George Carter, and rumor held that the other was Clark himself. The two men returned to the store the next night, having not learned from their close call, and were seen by the same neighbor, who called the police. By the time officers arrived, the housebreakers had decided to ply their trade elsewhere.

The coroner's jury returned a verdict of murder against Clark on August 17, even though he had not been located. George Carter was found guilty of being an accessory to murder. More legal bad news for the missing man came the next day when his wife, Della, decided that she no longer wanted to be Howard Clark's partner in times good and ill and filed for divorce.

Days passed with no trace of Clark. A widely circulated wanted poster included unflattering comments: "Is a sneaking coward; have information that he fainted…when notified of the death of the officer, then immediately fled the city…Can not look you in the face…Sullen look." In the days before easy reproduction of photographs, before fingerprinting and before DNA testing, wanted posters included laborious statistics measuring various portions of a criminal's anatomy. These were called Bertillon measurements after the French criminologist who popularized their use. Thus, Clark's wanted poster revealed his height and weight, as well as such minutiae as the exact dimensions of his head, feet and fingers. One assumes that the well-equipped policeman of 1898 carried calipers and a tape measure.

Some detectives were convinced Clark had slipped out of the city. Others thought that the roads, the departing trains and the waterfront were too closely watched to allow his escape and that he must be hiding in Louisville. There was a rash of Clark sightings among the nervous populace. He was seen repeatedly in the city, as well as in New Albany, St. Louis, Chicago and Nashville—not to mention other exotic locales such as Belleville, Illinois; Cementville, Indiana; and Utica, Indiana. It was alleged that he hid in Jeffersonville's pesthouse—a house where unfortunates with contagious diseases were quarantined. If true, it was a clever move since no detective in his right mind would willingly enter one.

Clark's fellow burglar George Carter had a preliminary hearing in police court on August 24. He testified that Clark had shot Patrolman Heffernan and convinced the judge that he (Carter) had only been in the wrong place at the wrong time. Mattie Mahoney admitted under oath that she had been living in sin with Clark and that he had come home with a bloody head on the night of the murder. He had told her of having a "scrap" with two policemen and thought he had shot one. He stayed a while and slipped away after she informed him the cops were outside. She claimed she had not seen him since. The judge dismissed Mattie, but not before advising her "to try to live a better life," according to a news account. No further action appears to have been taken against Carter.

On August 29, Clark's attorney, A.J. Speckert, told the police that his client had never left Louisville—in fact, he was still hiding with unnamed cronies who seemed blithely unconcerned that they could be charged with aiding and abetting. Speckert himself had been offered a $750 reward to reveal Clark's hiding place, but he refused. "I have replied to them that I am not in that kind of business. I shall not betray my client," he sniffed. Attorney-client privilege, you know. Speckert added, "He will surrender himself when I say the word. I will advise him to give himself up in about ten days or two weeks." Clark's capitulation was not forthcoming, so he must not have taken his lawyer's advice.

Naturally, the police did not intend to sit around and swap knives while waiting for Clark to surrender whenever the whim struck him. They must have doubted Speckert's claim that Clark was still in the city, since Police Chief Haager and Corporal Lapaille abandoned the mean streets of Louisville and went out of the state in disguise in order to collar their most wanted man. Haager dressed as an effete summer vacationer, complete with a golf cap and bowtie, while Lapaille wore the duds of a railroad switchman. The *Courier-Journal* ran a story describing the detectives' search—complete with illustrations of them in their disguises—which would seem to defeat the purpose, since criminals and their attorneys read newspapers, too.

In mid-September came disturbing news: Mattie Mahoney had vanished, and it did not require astounding deductive powers to figure out where she went. Just as Bonnie Parker could not stay away from Clyde Barrow, Mattie could not long resist Howard's doubtful charms.

Nothing certain was known of Howard Clark's movements until the night of October 7. Police in Owensboro, Daviess County, were reliably informed that Clark had been seen rowing a skiff on the Ohio River, accompanied by a young woman. Chief of Police Lyman Pierce and two officers hurried to the river and crossed in their own boat, hoping to beat Clark to the opposite shore and surprise him when he landed. Around 3:00 a.m., they saw the silhouette of an approaching skiff. The police rowed for it. Officer George Sherwood got close enough to seize the craft's front gunwale. Clark—for it was he—aimed a shotgun at Sherwood and said, "Drop that pistol in the river and bear off." Mattie, who had been lying in the bottom of the skiff, arose with a gun and pointed it at Sherwood's abdomen. The officers, realizing their predicament, unhanded Clark's boat and let it drift away into the darkness. They had not wanted to risk shooting a woman anyway. But they did sail back to Owensboro to organize a massive manhunt, and they alerted other towns on the river to keep a lookout for the fugitives.

Back in August, attorney Speckert had told the papers that he thought he would be able to clear Clark of the murder charge on the grounds that, according to Kentucky law, "a policeman has no right to search a man or arrest him unless he knows the man to be a felon or unless he sees that man commit a misdemeanor." Therefore, his client Clark shot in self-defense after Patrolman Heffernan belabored his head with a billy club. Speckert's theory, while rich in entertainment value, was misapplied. He did not take into account that Howard Clark was well known to the Louisville police force as a desperate crook; also, they caught Clark and Carter red-handed trying to burgle a store. Speckert never got a chance to attempt this novel defense in court because, like Bonnie and Clyde, Mattie and Howard were destined to end their brief lives riddled with bullets.

Their last day was October 9, just hours after the encounter on the river. Their final actions were traced afterward. Howard Clark and his deluded girlfriend abandoned the skiff and attempted to escape across land. They spent the night sleeping in a cornfield in Spencer County, Indiana, opposite Owensboro. They ate breakfast at Joe Yeager's farm. They tried to trick their pursuers by doubling back. At 11:00 a.m., three officers from Owensboro named Taylor, Bell and Mosely accidentally encountered the fugitives, who were sitting by the roadside under a tree—it was autumn, so no doubt its leaves were turning colors beautifully. Clark was dressed in rags; Mattie wore boy's clothes, a disguise attempted by numerous women in the long and sordid history of crime. As far as I can tell, it has never successfully fooled anyone even once.

Howard Clark was armed to the teeth, as the officers found out later when it was considerably safer to examine him. He was toting a .44-caliber Colt revolver, a breech-loading shotgun, a short-barreled .32-caliber revolver, bullets and a dirk. He shot three times at the officers with the .44-caliber pistol and then handed the weapon to Mattie as he scrambled for a shotgun. She managed to shoot once. None of the shots fired by Clark and Mahoney had any effect, but the surprised officers opened fire with two shotguns and a rifle. Both fugitives were struck several times. Before she received her fatal wound, Mattie leaped in front of Howard to protect him from the volley. She died instantly with bullets lodged in her brain, heart, hand and arm. She managed to retain her looks even in death. A reporter noted, "A slight trace of blood on the cheek was the only mark which was plainly in evidence." No such luck for Howard, who lingered for three and a half hours, despite having parted company with the top of his head. The reporter graphically described Howard's less than pristine condition: "Clark's hair was clotted with blood and earth, and blood gushed from his lips and nostrils and gurgled in his throat as he lay in his death agony." As the Book of Proverbs says, the way of transgressors is hard.

The bodies lay where they fell for hours. Before the coroner came to spoil the fun, hundreds of people made the laborious trip from Owensboro to Indiana to see the infamous lovers stiffening with rigor mortis under the tree. The October 11 edition of the *Courier-Journal* included a drawing of this scene, but the artist chose to depict Mattie in a proper dress rather than boy's clothing.

Later in the day, authorities from Louisville came to retrieve the infamous corpses from a Rockport funeral home. They had to elbow their way through a crowd of several hundred who had come to see the bodies, a popular form of mass entertainment in the days before television. The police used those Bertillon measurements to ascertain that the dead man was in fact Howard Clark. Mattie was identified from

Howard and Mattie dead under the tree. The sketch artist omitted the gruesome details. *From the* Louisville Courier-Journal *of October 11, 1898. Reprinted courtesy of the* Courier-Journal.

photographs. Both were malnourished due to the difficulty of eating well while on the run. Clark's father requested that his son's body be shipped to Louisville for burial; Mattie's mother, who had accompanied the police to Indiana, tearfully stated that her daughter's corpse would have to be disposed of at Indiana's expense, as she had no funds to bring her home for a proper burial. Mrs. Mahoney cried, "I tried to keep her away from Clark but she would not mind." Later she added, bitterly, "I won't have the body brought home. I have not the money to spend for a funeral even if I had the inclination. Howard Clark caused her downfall. If his people want to bury her, they can. She disowned me. I'll have nothing to do with the body, even if she has been killed. Her full name was Mattie Belle Mahoney, and she was sixteen years old." True to Mrs. Mahoney's wishes, Mattie was laid to rest in Rockport. Mattie's seducer and number one bad influence, Howard Clark, was buried without ceremony in Louisville's Cave Hill Cemetery, where his remains mingle amongst those of his more reputable relations.

A hearing was held in Rockport on October 10, during which it was ruled that the Kentucky officers had acted justifiably when they shot Mattie and Howard. It was regretted that the young woman had been killed, but she had left the police no choice. The *Courier-Journal*'s editorialists disagreed, calling the shooting of Mattie "a shocking incident" and disclosing that she had been pregnant at the time of her death. "The man was as dangerous as a tiger at bay and should have been treated as such," thundered the writer, "but by no stretch of imagination could this child of sixteen be regarded as an enemy to be engaged in a duel to the death." Noting that her pistol was nothing compared to the policemen's shotguns, the sentimentalist at the *Courier-Journal* proclaimed that Mattie "was practically as defenseless as a sheep." A sheep that was shooting at us, the officers might have countered.

The rest of the sad story can be told in a few sentences. Della Clark's suit for divorce was dropped on the grounds that her husband was dead. After some dispute over legal technicalities, the Owensboro officers who had risked their lives facing Mattie and Howard were given the reward money. Hiram Young, a farmer who had been riding with the Owensboro police and had been an eyewitness to the shooting, claimed that Mattie was unarmed. But he had said just the opposite under oath during the original inquest, and it was remembered that Mattie had aimed a gun at a policeman's belly during the adventure on the river on her last night on earth. Few people believed Young, but the *Courier-Journal* used the occasion to run another editorial decrying "the reckless use of firearms" by officers.

9

The Course of True Love, Etc.

Back in the days when Mr. Cleveland was president and the newly discovered X-ray was all the rage, a lad named Charles J. Miller was dating Hattie McQuistion. She has been described as "quite pretty" and a sharp dresser. Both were in their late teens and dwelt in Parkland, a suburb of Louisville. All went well until Hattie got pregnant and Charles refused to marry her. She gave birth on Sunday, August 23, 1896; Charles fled Parkland the following Thursday. Hattie was not one to take such an affront lightly, and in February 1897, she had Miller hauled into criminal court on charges of criminal seduction.

Anyone who has done jury duty knows that, generally speaking, it is less fun than tweezing ingrown hairs but more fun than getting killed. In this case, however, the lucky jury had choice seats at the best show in Louisville. The trial was a sensation, and every day the courtroom was as packed as though a three-legged chicken were on display. A reporter declared that the case "attracted the largest crowd perhaps ever seen in the Criminal division"—so large that both courtroom doors were left open and the hallway outside was crammed with people curious to see the wheels of justice turn and also out to get a cheap thrill while they were at it. The *Louisville Commercial* said there wasn't even standing room.

The love letters that passed between Charles and Hattie—150 of them—were read aloud as evidence, leaving both defendant and plaintiff petrified with embarrassment. The formerly love-struck couple's saccharine names for each other became a matter of legal

Above, left: Charles Miller. *From the* Louisville Commercial *of February 6, 1897.*

Above, right: Hattie McQuistion. *From the* Louisville Commercial *of February 6, 1897.*

record, including "Darling," "Love," "Little Love," "Ma Honey," "Sweet One," "Pet" and "My Darling Loved One—Dearest Pet." In one, Hattie declared that she loved Charlie better than "cakes and pie." She had also composed a poem for her fair-weather boyfriend:

> *As sure as the vine grows round the stump*
> *I love you better than a sugar lump.*

Hattie and Charles signed their letters with arcane initials, thus enjoying their own secret language of love. Charles ended one missive with "S.W.A.K.B. B.S.O.S.Y.K.Y.M.D.Y.U.D." A second concluded with the initials "B.A.T.Z." For her part, Hattie signed one "S.W.D.K.—B.B.S.O.C.Y.K." and another "B.B.S.O.C.Y.K.—S.W.A.K.—Y.M.D.Y.U.D.—S.M.A.K.S.O." (S.W.A.K. obviously meant "Sealed with a Kiss," but the only other acronym that was ever explained was G.B.D.B.—"Good Bye Darling Boy." The others must be mysteries forever, like Stonehenge.) Louisville newspapers refused to print the really scandalous testimony, so the sentimental gushiness was the hottest stuff their readers would get. The *Louisville Times* noted that "[o]ne point in the defense involves a very unusual scientific question" and then cheated posterity by refusing to state what that question was.

When attorney Aaron Kohn, representing Charles Miller, started cross-examination, he declared that all ladies and gentlemen should leave the courtroom because he would not gloss over any sordid details in his efforts to get to the truth. Naturally, nobody left the room. Hattie wept a lot, which probably helped her case.

Charles Miller took the stand on February 5. He denied having seduced Hattie and denied that he had promised to marry her. In the days before blood typing and DNA, paternity cases were settled by juries—and the chivalrous all-male juries of the era tended to side with weeping women. If this particular jury found Miller guilty, he could face between one and five years in jail.

The judge considered the evidence presented on February 7 so ribald that he permitted no one in the courtroom but the jury, witnesses and attorneys. Whatever this evidence was, it did not bode well for Charles Miller. The

A valentine from Charles to Hattie, entered as court evidence. *From the* Louisville Commercial *of February 7, 1897.*

What could have been. *From the* Louisville Commercial *of February 9, 1897.*

next day, the jury found him guilty and sentenced him to one year in the penitentiary. "I will go to the penitentiary for twenty years before I will marry her," declared Miller.

"I don't blame you," said his attorney, Mr. Kohn.

But the reality of facing a year in the slammer must have changed Miller's mind. On February 9, he married Hattie in the jailhouse, and afterward the

And what actually happened. *From the* Louisville Commercial *of February 10, 1897.*

case against him was dismissed. Miller protested all the while that he was not guilty. "The wedding," remarked the *Courier-Journal*, "was by no means a joyful affair…The contracting parties treated each other with scant courtesy." The *Times* concurred that the ceremony "was very brief. Neither bride nor groom spoke to each other, and only nodded their assent to the formal questions propounded by the officiating magistrate." The *Commercial's* reporter noticed that they held hands "in a rather constrained manner" and added, "Miller looked very much as though he would rather be playing marbles, while the girl's face betokened disgust." The none-too-happy couple stated they would not live together. Perhaps they changed their minds later—perhaps.

So, if any descendants of Charles J. Miller and Hattie McQuistion are reading these words, this is how your ancestors met.

10

Striking a Blow
for the Workingman

We have a criminal jury system which is superior to any in the world; and its efficiency is only marred by the difficulty in finding twelve men every day who don't know anything and can't read. And I may observe that we have an insanity plea that would have saved Cain.
—Mark Twain, 1875

All too often we hear on the news about the latest shooting in the workplace, and we comfort ourselves with the fiction that such things didn't happen "in the good old days." A quick look at some newspapers from yesteryear will teach us otherwise.

Take, for example, the incident that occurred shortly before noon on July 6, 1903, at Louisville's Union Station, located at Tenth and Broadway. Pulaski Leeds, superintendent of machinery for the Louisville & Nashville Railroad and considered "one of the best-known railroad men in the South," was at his desk in his third-floor office. Several employees milled about, so there was no shortage of witnesses to what happened next. The door swung open, and in stepped forty-one-year-old George B. Warner, an electrician who had worked for the L&N for two years. In January 1903, Leeds had sent Warner to manage the railroad's electrical works in Decatur, Alabama, but had him recalled to Louisville for performing unsatisfactorily. Warner was offered another L&N job in a location of less importance, but he declined to accept it and had been looking for a job ever since. Warner seemed to hold no grudge against his former boss, who had even promised to help Warner find another position.

(Warner thought he was entitled to keep his job even if he wasn't very good at it or, failing that, that he was entitled to a misleading glowing letter of recommendation. Nothing is more dangerous than a sense of entitlement.)

Now, on this blazing July day, Warner said that he needed to see Leeds on an urgent matter. Stenographer T.N. Dolson told Warner that he would have to wait until Leeds finished writing a letter. Warner cheerfully agreed and took a seat.

Ten minutes later, Leeds completed his task. Warner came to the desk and asked if Leeds would write a letter of recommendation for him. Leeds replied that that would be against company policy but added that he would be glad to provide a spoken recommendation to any of Warner's prospective employers. This answer did not satisfy Warner, who erupted with a poor substitution of invective for reasoning. "Well, damn you and your recommendation," he cried. "You can take it and go to hell with it!" He punctuated his statement by drawing a .38-caliber revolver from his hip pocket and shooting Leeds in the chest and jaw; the second bullet exited through the back of the superintendent's head. Then Warner shot himself behind the left ear. It all happened so quickly that the clerks in the room barely had time to comprehend it.

Leeds's employees called in doctors. The injured man remained conscious and said, "I am not hurt much, and will be all right shortly." He added, "I cannot understand the reason for the attack. I had just finished telling Warner that I would be glad to help him in any way possible when he fired at me." Doctors cautioned him not to speak, and he answered further questions by nodding or shaking his head. The assassin, too, was alive, and both men were taken to their respective hospitals.

The *Courier-Journal*'s July 7 headline read: "Mr. Leeds Will Recover… His Assailant May Die." Both assertions were perfectly wrong. Leeds died late at night on July 8, while Warner slowly recovered from the nasty self-inflicted gunshot wound. His skull was fractured, but somehow he had missed his brain. Mr. Leeds's funeral at Cave Hill Cemetery was largely attended, not only by L&N big shots but also by his subordinates, who were heartbroken that their beloved chief was dead. It required two special trains to accommodate the mourners from out of town. Hundreds had to be turned away from the church where Leeds's funeral services were held due to lack of space. Two thousand railroad workmen held a meeting to pass a resolution expressing their grief. Milton Smith, president of the L&N, said, "Mr. Leeds was the last of all our department men to give affront to an employee, however humble." George Evans, the railroad's general manager,

Warner shoots Leeds in the latter's office. *From the* Louisville Courier-Journal *of July 7, 1903. Reprinted courtesy of the* Courier-Journal.

called Leeds "one of the kindest-hearted men I ever knew. I know of no injury he ever intended to anyone." Everyone involved with the company said the same.

By committing his rash act of vengeance, George Warner made himself so exceedingly unpopular that plainclothes detectives were assigned to guard him at City Hospital. But there was one person who bore him no malice. Dr. George Griffiths, one of Leeds's attending physicians, stated that his patient was of such a kindly disposition that even as he lay dying he was concerned with his assassin's welfare. "How is Warner?" he had asked. "I do hope that he will get well." (Just after he had been shot, Leeds urged bystanders to tend to Warner's wounds first.) Warner had one friend other than the man he had killed: his wife, who traveled from Beaver Springs, Pennsylvania, to attend to him as he recovered.

Not surprisingly, the coroner's jury determined that Leeds's death was a murder when it convened on July 13. Warner would have to stand trial when physically fit. Because his health was precarious, his doctors thought it wise not to tell him that his victim had died, lest the excitement of knowing that he would be tried for murder should prove too much for him or that he might complete his bungled suicide attempt. The doctors even denied Warner access to newspapers; somehow he managed to get hold of an issue announcing the death of Leeds but was unable to read it due to his head injury. He was using the newspaper to fan away houseflies. It wasn't until July 23 that the authorities, informed that Warner had regained his strength, finally told him that he was officially and legally a murderer. His response was an unemotional "Is that so?" He was taken from his hospital room to a jail cell.

It is likely that the defense lawyers of Louisville were not clamoring to represent Warner because he was not defendable. His friends stated that he was not in the habit of carrying a concealed weapon, so it was evident that the shooting was premeditated. When Warner came to the L&N office that day, he had every intention of shooting his former employer. Also, physicians did not see any signs of madness; he was described as having "a remarkably clear mind" and being "at all times rational, never suggesting the slightest form of insanity." Four eyewitnesses who had been in Leeds's office swore that the shooting was unprovoked. One of the few voices speaking on Warner's behalf was that of his wife, who found it impossible to believe he would shoot another man without reason. She was convinced, based more on loyalty than the facts, that the by-all-accounts gentlemanly and kind Pulaski Leeds must have goaded her husband to his breaking point and Warner killed his tormentor in the heat of the moment—with the brand-new revolver that he was not known to have previously carried. The deep pockets of the L&N Railroad hired Aaron Kohn, one of Louisville's best prosecutors, to assist the commonwealth's attorney, Joseph Huffaker. Their avowed goal was to send Warner to the gallows.

Despite this unpromising start, attorney R. Lee Suter defended Warner. His strategy was revealed early in the preliminary trial, held at the end of July: he would try to prove that Warner was temporarily deranged. The insanity defense in general, and the *temporary* insanity defense in particular, is one of the oldest legal tricks in the book; then, as now, it was too often used to save patently sane criminals from getting their just desserts. To be fair to Suter, under the circumstances the insanity plea was one of the few legal defenses open to his client. A single juror afflicted with a soft heart or gullibility is all that is required to result in a hung jury. There are risks involved with pleading temporary insanity, of course. It is difficult to prove, and the plea has been the means of getting so many murderers off scot-free over the years that jurors are suspicious of it, if not actively hostile toward it.

Despite Suter's objections, Warner was indicted for murder on the last day of September. Bail was denied, so he would have to stew in jail until his trial began. While he waited, his rash act of violence resulted in a second fatality, this one unintentional. On October 4, Warner's sixteen-year-old son, George Jr., died at Logansport, Indiana, of grief (or so the papers said) caused by the disgrace his father had brought on the family. Another son, Edward, would die from the same cause in Butte, Montana, in February 1906.

Warner's trial was to begin on November 30, but his attorneys, Suter and Jacob Solinger, won a continuance until February 3, 1904. "We prefer to wait and develop our defense in the courtroom," Mr. Solinger told a reporter on the morning of the trial's first day, which sounds perilously close to an admission that he and Mr. Suter had no earthly idea how they were going to save their client's neck and would have to make up their strategy as they went. The *Courier-Journal* speculated that they were trying to "[keep] the prosecution in the dark as long as possible as to the position of the defense," but it was hardly a stunning surprise when the defense played the insanity card as expected. In addition to casting doubt on Warner's mental state, which they claimed was precarious because he had been blacklisted from the L&N—presumably by Leeds, though they had no evidence to support such a contention—and thus had been unable to find work, the defense split hairs with the witnesses. They asked whether Warner had demanded "a" letter, "the" letter or "that" letter. Suter and Solinger were suggesting that Leeds had letters of recommendation written by some unknown person, which he refused to give back to Warner.

On the second day of the trial, Warner took the stand and claimed that he had met Mr. Leeds on the street a couple days before the murder, and Leeds had privately admitted that Warner had been blacklisted. Warner added that he had not cursed at Mr. Leeds before firing—never mind what all those eyewitnesses said. He described the mundane events of July 6, 1903, with needle-sharp clarity—yet somehow his memory became conveniently fuzzy when he described the most significant part of that day. Warner said that his mind had gone blank when he entered Leeds's office; therefore, he was insane and could be held responsible for nothing: "I did not know I had killed anyone until taken to jail." Warner added that his maternal grandmother, his uncle and his uncle's two children were all crazy. Gilding the lily, attorney Suter elaborated that Warner had survived an electric shock of 2,500 volts and had not been the same ever since. The prosecution produced witnesses who testified that they had heard Warner promising he would kill Leeds. This testimony was a two-edged sword: it could indicate that his crime was premeditated and carefully planned, but it could also be interpreted as evidence that Warner was insane. It is more probable, of course, that Warner was sane and simply allowed his temper to get the better of him, but that isn't the kind of thing that wins an acquittal.

Warner contradicted his acquaintances by stating that he was in the habit of carrying a pistol. Co-prosecutor Kohn got Warner to confess that he had purchased the gun with which he killed Leeds on the morning of the shooting. Attempts were made to blame the victim. The defense implied that Leeds had blacklisted Warner, and thus the latter was driven over the edge by his desperation to find work to support his family.

The next day, doctors took the stand and offered wildly varying expert testimony regarding the prisoner's mental condition. Some doctors believed Warner to be completely sane, while others thought he was—to use the medically accurate term—totally nuts. The jurors agreed that he was of sound mind and, on February 6, found Warner guilty, despite the defense's attempts in its closing argument to compare Warner to Charles Guiteau, insane assassin of President Garfield, and to paint the condemned man as a hapless victim of the flint-hearted L&N Railroad. (As in modern times, corporations that commit the unthinkable crime of daring to make a profit—and, by doing so, keep so many of us gainfully employed—always make handy villains among demagogues and the unthinking.) The jurors recommended that Warner be hanged. He seemed distinctly unconcerned.

Defense attorneys Suter and Solinger filed a motion for a new trial on the grounds that the judge had not informed the jury that it had the option of finding Warner guilty of manslaughter—a verdict that would have gotten their client only two to twenty-one years in the slammer. As Warner waited for the judge's decision, a contemporary news article described his calmness: "At the jail he is regarded with curiosity, so strange is his attitude compared to that of his fellow prisoners." His sang-froid was unbroken by the double dose of bad news, which came on March 19, that the judge had denied Warner a new trial and that he would be hanged on April 29.

Suter and Solinger appealed the decision, which bought Warner more time in this sweet, sweet world. The net result was that, with more time to think over the predicament he had gotten himself into, Warner finally lost his stoicism. On May 15—the one-year anniversary of the hanging of John Black, who had murdered his uncle Archie James—Warner reportedly was "in a state of utter humility."

While waiting for the end, Warner spent his time engaging in activities ranging from bizarre to heroic to unwholesome to heartwarming. The bizarre moment came when his attorney R. Lee Suter was shot to death by W.O. Vaughn at Louisville's Dream Palace fishing camp on July 3, 1904. Warner claimed to have seen the tragedy enacted in a prophetic nightmare full of symbolism that would have delighted Freud. In the dream, he saw Suter coated with blood in a wooded area and with "a great red stream flowing high in the air over his body." The lawyer assured Warner by saying, "I am not much hurt. I'll be there to defend you till hell freezes over." Standing nearby was a blindfolded woman holding a pair of scales, and behind her stood a gallows. Warner's fellow prisoners affirmed that he had told them about the dream ten days before Suter was shot. Warner's heroic activity took place on August 22, when he protected an elderly and insane prisoner, Joseph Curley, from being beaten by David Hutchins. The unwholesome activity was Warner's failed attempt at suicide on October 14, when he produced a hidden razor and slashed his throat, wrist and leg in a jail bathtub, an activity frowned upon by the guards. The heartwarming moment was the October 15 meeting at the jailhouse with his brother J.D. Warner of Logansport, Indiana, whom the prisoner had not seen in five years. George said he was glad the guards had saved his life, swore he would never attempt suicide again and promised that if he must be hanged, he would march up those gallows steps like a manly man.

It looked as though Warner would have a chance to put his final assertion to the test. On February 1, 1905, a year after his trial, the court of appeals affirmed the Jefferson Criminal Court's original decision. Warner would be hanged, Governor J.C.W. Beckham to decide the date later. The city was constructing a swanky new jailhouse on Green Street, and it was said that Warner would be the first man hanged at it.

Something then happened that will be of interest to students of human nature: the city's laborers, apparently having forgotten what a great and kind boss Pulaski Leeds had been, started feeling sympathy for the same assassin they had desired to lynch a year and a half earlier. Labor unions made a hero out of Warner and raised money to help with his defense; they also gave the prisoner $500 to spend as he pleased. In the face of this support, Warner was convinced that his case eventually would be heard before the Supreme Court of the United States.

Attorney Suter was dead and in his grave and unable to help, no matter what he may have promised in Warner's dream, but Attorney Solinger was still plugging away. On March 1, he and attorney Colonel Bennett Young filed a petition to the court of appeals for a rehearing on the grounds that Warner's sanity should be tested. The court saw the wisdom in this and allowed them a two-week extension in which to file supplemental material arguing in favor of a rehearing. On a more personal level, George Warner's wife traveled from Logansport, Indiana, to Frankfort to visit him. She was ambitious and reportedly thought that he deserved, if not a full pardon with abject apologies, then at least a reduction of his sentence to life in prison.

On March 25, the court of appeals announced that it still saw no reason to interfere with the lower court's decision. The rehearing was denied. Unless the governor commuted the sentence, Warner would confront the noose at sunrise on May 19. Defense attorneys Solinger and Young took this as a cue to encourage anyone and everyone with an interest in seeing a murderer escape his just punishment to sign a petition asking that Warner's sentence be commuted on the grounds that "he was not a man of sound mind when he committed the murder." Members of labor unions across the state signed, as did prominent Louisville businessmen, concerned citizens and probably a few people who had swell new fountain pens they wanted to try out. By April 7, the defense had collected twenty thousand signatures; by April 29, twenty-five thousand. Labor unions expressed a fierce determination to collect fifty thousand. (One man who refused to sign when asked was George Looms, who had been foreman of the jury that convicted Warner. He maintained that their verdict was correct and just.) The number of persons who signed the petition was remarkable, considering that Warner's attorneys had not offered the slightest scrap of evidence that the beneficiary of all this kindness was innocent. It was not a case of reasonable doubt; there was no question that he had committed the crime, since he performed it in front of witnesses in broad daylight and shot himself afterward. Nor had the petitioners received any evidence that Warner was insane; once the trial was over and Warner was in jail, he dropped the crazy act and spoke as reasonably as you please.

Governor Beckham was not swayed by the petition. On May 11, he announced that Warner would be hanged as scheduled. The prisoner was resigned to his fate, and to a reporter he "willingly recounted all the incidents of the murder"—which, the reader will recall, he mysteriously had been unable to remember under oath. Warner added that he was not sorry for what he had done:

If I had the deed to do over again, I would not flinch from my purpose. Leeds had refused to return my letters of recommendation, which were the only possible means by which I could secure a new position after I had been discharged from the employ of the L and N, and finding that I had no means of supporting my wife and family, life did not seem worth living to me.

He did not explain why he thought he could provide for his family by shooting another man and then himself, thereby ensuring that he would be either dead or imprisoned for life. Warner declared that by killing Leeds he had struck a blow for the workingman, a statement that undoubtedly warmed the hearts of the labor union members who were holding mass meetings on his behalf and who came to his cell to offer him company, moral support and treats. Perhaps they took time off from work to do these things.

Governor Beckham signed the death warrant and sent it to Sheriff E.T. Schmitt. Warner's attorneys were nothing if not persistent. On May 13, they announced that if the governor refused to commute the prisoner's sentence, they would ask the courts to appoint a commission to examine his sanity. Warner, not surprisingly, agreed that he was crazy—or at least had been temporarily. Six days before he was to be hanged, Warner told a reporter, "When I committed the deed I must have been beside myself. I could not have done such a thing willfully. A man, you know, can be driven beyond the limit of endurance. I am sorry now that I committed the act."

A committee of sixty men, "composed of representatives of every organized craft in the city of Louisville and the State of Kentucky," planned to travel to Frankfort to see the governor in person. This committee was to go by special train car. It would have been a rich irony if transportation had been supplied by the L&N, but it was a C&O car. The governor was not scheduled in Frankfort on May 15, the day the committee intended to make its trip, so it resolved to pester him when he came to Louisville.

As late as May 16—three days before the scheduled hanging—Governor Beckham refused to interfere. He went over the details of the Warner case carefully and was "convinced that it is not one deserving clemency." It was time for Warner's attorneys to unveil Plan B. Solinger and Bennett asked Sheriff Schmitt to institute an insanity inquiry. Warner spent the day smoking cigars while pacing in his cell. He telegraphed his wife in Logansport and asked her to visit him for the last time. Bring our three children, he said. His friends continued to consult with defense attorney Solinger and hope for a miracle.

Then came a delightful stroke of luck for those who would see Warner escape the gallows. After Sheriff Schmitt read affidavits written by jailer John Pflanz, prison evangelist George Herr and labor leader J.H. Tierney—all of whom believed Warner was insane—he agreed to impanel a jury of twelve to determine the truth. The reader will note a flaw in the logic behind the proceedings: the question that should have been explored was not whether Warner was insane in May 1905 but whether he was insane on July 6, 1903, when he killed Pulaski Leeds.

The hearing was held on May 18; on the same day, workers constructed the scaffold in the jail yard. Since the trial had been cobbled together quickly, the prosecution did not have time to provide proof of the prisoner's sanity and had only a few witnesses. As a result, the weight of evidence was heavily in favor of the defense. The judge who had presided over Warner's trial in 1903 listened to the testimony as a spectator and thought Warner was insane. He telegraphed a recommendation of clemency to Governor Beckham. The governor received a similar message from Dr. Ellis Duncan, the physician who had watched over the prisoner as he convalesced in the hospital after shooting Leeds and himself. Sheriff Schmitt and even commonwealth's attorney Joe Huffaker thought a respite to further examine the prisoner's state of mind was in order. The governor received one hundred telegrams "from all walks of life" urging him to be merciful. Warner's small daughter was allowed to sit on his knee and stare at the jury during the courtroom proceedings, but I'm sure that didn't influence the trial in any way.

Warner, survivor of a self-inflicted gunshot to the head, got lucky again. After deliberating, the jury was deadlocked. Another insanity trial would have to be held. The news of Warner's stay of execution was cheered by people who had gathered inside the courthouse and six thousand more outside. Warner, his family, his attorneys and the labor unions were ecstatic. Pulaski Leeds's family was not. The jubilation cooled when people realized that Governor Beckham's act of clemency was conditional at best: should Warner be found sane by the second jury, he would be hanged on May 31. The best he could hope for was to spend the rest of his life in an insane asylum, since Beckham had vowed he would never commute the sentence or grant a pardon.

Interestingly, the jury members who thought Warner was crazy felt that it was *a result of his having shot himself in the head*, which did not answer the pertinent question as to whether he had been insane *before* shooting himself. It will be remembered, too, that Warner had fractured his skull but sustained no damage to his brain. Warner sounded perfectly sane and rational in a *Courier-Journal* interview conducted after the court made its announcement.

During Warner's respite, Governor Beckham continued to receive letters and telegrams from citizens, laborers and defense attorneys asking him to appeal the prisoner's sentence.

The second inquest into Warner's sanity was held on May 27. "I wish it were all over," he remarked. None of the three doctors summoned by the prosecution made an appearance. The proceedings were brief and to the point, and the jury took merely four minutes to decide that Warner was a lunatic—despite his lack of brain damage and the dearth of convincing evidence that he had been crazy before, during or after his murder of Pulaski Leeds. According to the *Courier-Journal*, the verdict "was received with wild enthusiasm by the two or three thousand of Warner's sympathizers, mostly union labor men, who crowded the courtroom and Court Place." Prosecutor Joe Huffaker remarked sourly, "If the Commonwealth had had a barrel of money at its back with which to engage expert witnesses, it could have produced as much testimony upholding Warner's sanity as was brought out against it."

The scaffold was dismantled on May 29. It was never used again at the old Louisville jail, the new prison on Green Street being opened for business in June. The same gallows was reassembled in January 1906 and used to hang William Van Dalsen, slasher of his girlfriend's throat.

On June 1, Warner was sent to the Western Asylum for the Insane at Hopkinsville. Instead of being grateful that he had escaped execution, Warner was miffed because he had had his heart set on being sent to the Central Asylum at Lakeland. Despite Governor Beckham's vow to the contrary, he commuted Warner's sentence to life in prison, which meant that if the prisoner were ever released from the goof-works, he would spend the rest of his days in the penitentiary. Meanwhile, prosecutor Aaron Kohn, who had done his duty in trying to keep a potentially dangerous man off the streets, received an anonymous letter, notable for its superb spelling and construction, threatening to kill either him or his son—the authors were not particular. It was signed "Committee."

At the asylum, Warner distinguished himself by showing no symptoms whatsoever of insanity. He had been locked away from society—forever, it appeared. Surely some of the thousands of people who worked to have him declared insane so that he might dodge the gallows must have questioned whether they had done the right thing. Was Warner, after all, truly deranged or just shamming? If anyone wondered about this, they got their answer only four months after he was sent to the Western Asylum. On the night of October 23, 1905, the supposedly insane Warner displayed considerable mechanical ingenuity by removing the iron plate on the door and picking the lock. He removed his clothes from a peg outside the door and cleverly replaced them with another inmate's clothing. He picked the lock on the outer hallway door and escaped into the night via the institution's basement, showing further evidence of his sound common sense by foiling all of his pursuers. Telephones and telegraphs alerted the police in every town in a hundred-mile radius, but Warner had escaped without leaving so much as a footprint. Even a $500 reward failed to turn up a single clue. The so-called crazy man had made perfect asses of his defense attorneys, twelve jurors, assorted jail officials, nine doctors who testified that he was insane, labor unions who had made it their pet project to get him released rather than tend to their own spheres of business and at least twenty-five thousand petition signers.

On April 18, 1910, after nearly five years of freedom, George B. Warner—who had been using the disappointingly uncreative pseudonym George Wagner—turned himself in to the sheriff of Deer Lodge, Montana. He said he was tired of running. As proof that some people never learn, before he was extradited to Kentucky there was talk of forming a petition asking for his pardon in the event that he went to prison.

Warner arrived back in the Bluegrass State on the last day of April. He would not face the death penalty, his sentence having been commuted to life in prison before he broke out of the asylum; even so, he did not end up in the penitentiary. He was returned to the asylum at Hopkinsville. On the way there, Warner and Deputy Sheriff Robert Kaltenbacher spent the night in the jail at Louisville, the city where the prisoner had killed his man. Warner informed reporters that he spent time on the lam in Chicago, British Columbia, Seattle, China, Japan, San Francisco, Honolulu, Cuba, New Orleans and, finally, the American West, where he settled at Deer Lodge. He claimed that he had suffered from constant pain in his head due to his self-inflicted gunshot wound. One night, after taking a few drinks in a saloon, he decided to give himself up to the authorities: "I did not care for freedom if I had to feel as though every man that I met knew that I was a hunted man. In fact, I could hardly look a man straight in the face." He complained that he had not heard from his wife and children in years.

The *Courier-Journal* editorialized that the Warner case was a perfect illustration of "the absurdity of the insanity plea" and argued that the culprit should go straight to jail, not back to the asylum. Nevertheless, on May 4, George Warner arrived at the Western Asylum ready and eager, it seemed, to do penance for murdering Pulaski Leeds. It was announced the next day that the Commonwealth of Kentucky, evidently having not learned its lesson before, would hold another inquest into Warner's sanity.

Warner had other ideas, though, and on June 30 he again picked the lock on his cell door, again escaped the asylum and again vanished. Superintendent Dr. T.W. Gardiner "expressed great regret" over the escape; guard John W. Miller, who had been reading or napping when the inmate got away, was fired for negligence.

This time around, Warner's conscience did not trouble him. He was never seen again.

Acknowledgements

Laura All; Geneta Chumley; Drema Colangelo; Gaile Sheppard Dempsey; Eastern Kentucky University Department of English and Theatre; Eastern Kentucky University Interlibrary Loan Department; Rosie Garcia; Ken Grimm; Amy and Quentin Hawkins; Will McKay and everyone at The History Press; Darrell and Swecia McQueen; Darren and Alison McQueen; Kyle and Bonnie (Bonty) McQueen; Michael, Lori and Blaine McQueen and Evan Holbrook; Lee Mitchum; Pat New; John Newman; Mark Taflinger and the *Louisville Courier-Journal*; Mia Temple. Also: The Comforter.

This book was edited by Lee Mitchum.

Bibliography

THE HANGED BUTCHER'S ALLEGED REJUVENATION

Louisville Commercial. "From Death to Life." January 26, 1870, 4.

———. "Minor Locals." January 28, 1870, 4.

Louisville Courier-Journal. "Absurd Rumor." January 27, 1870, 4.

———. "The Details of the Execution." Editorial. January 22, 1870, 2.

———. "A Fearful Gallows Scene." January 20, 1870, 1.

———. "The Kriel Show." January 22, 1870, 1.

———. "The Last of Kriel." January 21, 1870, 4.

———. "The Late Execution." January 25, 1870, 1.

———. "Scaffold and Halter." January 22, 1870, 4.

———. "We Publish Elsewhere a Communication." Editorial. January 22, 1870, 2.

———. "William Kreil [*sic*]." January 16, 1870, 4.

Louisville Daily Courier. "Local Odds and Ends." March 12, 1868, 3.

Louisville Daily Journal. "A Horrible Tragedy." March 8, 1868, 3.

———. "Local Budget." March 11, 1868, 2.

———. "Local Budget." March 14, 1868, 2.

———. "Local Budget." March 19, 1868, 2.

———. "The Murdered Wife." March 10, 1868, 2.

THE DIZZY BLONDES COME TO TOWN

Louisville Courier-Journal. "Attractions in the Theaters." December 10, 1923, 8.
———. "Attractions in the Theaters." December 13, 1923, 13.
———. "The Dizzy Blondes." May 25, 1878, 3.
———. "Dizzy Blondes at Library Hall." November 18, 1877, 1.
———. "Dizzy Blondes at Library Hall." November 20, 1877, 1.
———. "Electric Light." November 17, 1881, 8.
———. "Jeffersonville." November 25, 1877, 2.
———. "Kentucky News." November 8, 1877, 2.
———. "Local Brevities." December 3, 1877, 4.
———. "Local Brevities." January 6, 1878, 4.
———. "Mme. Duclos' Blondes." November 21, 1877, 4.
———. "Personal." November 27, 1877, 3.
———. "Police Slap Lid on Gayety Show." December 10, 1923, 1.
———. "A Slim Hall." November 21, 1877, 1.

CHESTNUT STREET'S HOUSE OF HORRORS

Louisville Courier-Journal. "Brownfield's Accounts." November 10, 1887, 5.
———. "Friday's Tragedy." November 7, 1887, 6.
———. "Gossip of the Day." November 16, 1887, 5.
———. "Gossip of the Day." December 15, 1887, 8.
———. "In the Grave." November 6, 1887, 11.
———. "Slaughter!" November 5, 1887, 1+.

CARRIE MCBRIDE, THE PUGILISTIC PROSTITUTE

Louisville Courier-Journal. "Carrie McBride." July 14, 1896, 7.
———. "Carrie McBride Leaves." May 12, 1889, 9.
———. "Carrie McBride to Answer." August 16, 1888, 8.
———. "Carrie McBride's Crime." June 11, 1888, 8.
———. "Carrie McBride's Last Battle." October 2, 1889, 6.
———. "Carrie McBride's Latest." March 26, 1890, 6.
———. "Carrie McBride's Muscle." April 15, 1889, 6.
———. "Carrie McBride's Snake." June 7, 1896, Section II, 4.
———. "Carrie McBride's Troubles." January 19, 1896, Section I, 4.

———. "Crime's End Draws Nigh." March 3, 1888, 8.
———. "The Notorious Carrie McBride." August 12, 1888, 2.
———. "A Notorious Character Gone." December 20, 1888, 6.
———. "She Loves Louisville." January 15, 1892, 8.
———. "Wretched Was the Life of Poor Carrie McBride." July 15, 1896, 8.

MURDER WILL NOT ALWAYS OUT

Louisville Courier-Journal. "Clews to the Crime." September 16, 1892, 6.
———. "Death and Shame." September 10, 1892, 8.
———. "Dismissed." September 22, 1892, 6.
———. "The End Yet Far Off." September 18, 1892, 4.
———. "He Was the Man." September 13, 1892, 6.
———. "Inquest Into the Poisoning." September 17, 1892, 8.
———. "Known in Louisville." November 27, 1892, 3.
———. "Mrs. Austin's Furniture." September 30, 1892, 8.
———. "New Evidence." September 19, 1892, 6.
———. "A Plot for Sardou." September 15, 1892, 4.
———. "The Poisoning Mystery." September 14, 1892, 8.
———. "A Puzzling Case." Editorial. September 19, 1892, 4.
———. "The Second Street Murder Mystery." Editorial. September 18, 1892, 16.
———. "Still a Mystery." September 12, 1892, 6.
———. "Suspicion." September 11, 1892, 3.
———. "Trails Are Cold." September 20, 1892, 8.
———. "Witness Johnson Arrives." September 21, 1892, 8.

YOUR FRIENDLY NEIGHBORHOOD PORNOGRAPHER

Louisville Courier-Journal. "After the Photographer." March 5, 1894, 8.
———. "Against Obscene Pictures." December 15, 1893, 8.
———. "Demands an Explanation." December 17, 1894, 6.
———. "Henry Zink Dead." April 2, 1896, 10.
———. "Henry Zink Is Free." December 10, 1894, 6.
———. "Henry Zink Pardoned." December 7, 1894, 6.
———. "Henry Zink Will Die Sure Now." December 28, 1894, 5.
———. "Investigating: The President Clearly Annoyed." December 15, 1894, 6.
———. "The Louisville Police Deny." November 20, 1893, 1.

———. "Nothing Will Be Done." November 20, 1893, 4.

———. "Not Much Like a Consumptive." December 13, 1894, 6.

———. "Photographer May Be Indicted." March 3, 1894, 8.

———. "'Pointer' for Police." November 21, 1893, 7.

———. "Says Zink Has Consumption." December 14, 1894, 5.

———. "Set For April 9." March 8, 1894, 8.

———. "Sports Get Bibles for Their Dollars." January 17, 1901, 4.

———. "Suppress It." November 26, 1893, 11.

———. "Surely Had the Consumption." December 18, 1894, 7.

———. "Thought It Was Something Bad." March 5, 1900, 4.

———. "Wants the Sentence Modified." March 6, 1894, 8.

———. "When the Louisville Police Search." Editorial. November 22, 1893, 4.

———. "Zink Begs for Mercy." March 1, 1894, 6.

———. "Zink Flees." November 19, 1893, 9.

———. "Zink Has Returned." November 23, 1893, 6.

———. "Zink's Case Postponed." March 18, 1894, 12.

———. "Zink's Punishment." March 2, 1894, 8.

———. "Zink Trapped." November 18, 1893, 1.

What Came of a Marriage between a Murderer and a Prostitute

Louisville Courier-Journal. "Bert Wing Makes Escape." January 7, 1908, 1+.

———. "Bert Wing Once More in State Reformatory." May 1, 1914, 3.

———. "Bert Wing's Trial." November 17, 1892, 8.

———. "Butchered." November 2, 1892, 1.

———. "Captured." November 11, 1892, 2.

———. "Charles Wing in Town." May 26, 1894, 12.

———. "The Fugitive." Editorial. May 4, 1914, 4.

———. "'Lifer' and 'Trusty.'" Editorial. May 1, 1914, 4.

———. "Negro Who Escaped with Wing Caught." January 12, 1908, IV, 3.

———. "Plans Suicide to Last Detail." March 27, 1908, 1.

———. "Said to Have Aided Bert Wing to Escape." February 7, 1908, 1.

———. "Says Trusties Carried Keys." April 30, 1914, 7.

———. "Still Free." November 3, 1892, 5.

———. "Stripped of His Clothes and Beaten." January 8, 1908, 3.

———. "Ubiquitous Wing." November 4, 1892, 5.

———. "Wing Finds a Friend." November 20, 1892, 3.

———. "Wing Pardoned." February 12, 1916, 3.

———. "Wing's Successful Flight." November 5, 1892, 3.

———. "Wing Tells His Story." November 16, 1892, 8.

LOUISVILLE'S BONNIE AND CLYDE

Louisville Courier-Journal. "A Bad Man." December 11, 1897, 4.

———. "Burglars Try to Rob a West End Grocery." August 17, 1898, 3.

———. "Clark in Louisville." August 22, 1898, 5.

———. "Clings to Her Lover." December 6, 1897, 8.

———. "Dark for Clark." August 25, 1898, 8.

———. "Ended by Death." October 16, 1898, II, 2.

———. "Found." November 24, 1897, 3.

———. "Go Free." October 11, 1898, 2.

———. "Grand Jury." October 22, 1898, 4.

———. "Hiding Here." August 30, 1898, 10.

———. "Insured in the Heptasophs." August 21, 1898, I, 8.

———. "Is It Clark?" August 24, 1898, 4.

———. "Is Located." October 9, 1898, II, 5.

———. "'Like a Father,' Howard Clark Says He Treated Maymie Mahoney." November 26, 1897, 2.

———. "Met in Jail." August 16, 1898, 5.

———. "No Trace of the Whereabouts of Maymie Mahoney." November 23, 1897, 8.

———. "No Word Comes from Col. Haager." September 2, 1898, 8.

———. "Price On His Head." August 25, 1898, 8.

———. "Riddled to Death with Bullets." October 10, 1898, 1+.

———. "Search for Howard Clark." August 20, 1898, 9.

———. "A Shocking Incident." Editorial. October 12, 1898, 4.

———. "Shot Down." August 13, 1898, 9.

———. "Slips Away Again." September 16, 1898, 4.

———. "Step Toward Freedom." August 26, 1898, 8.

———. "Succumbed." August 15, 1898, 4.

———. "Trouble Ahead." October 13, 1898, 9.

———. "Unchanged Is Patrolman Joseph Heffernan's Condition." August 14, 1898, II, 3.

———. "Vain Search for Clark." September 14, 1898, 4.

———. "Verdict of Murder." August 18, 1898, 7.

———. "Visited a Camp." September 4, 1898, I, 4.

———. "Wants a Divorce." August 19, 1898, 8.

———. "Was It Howard Clark?" September 24, 1898, 3.

———. "Where Good Work May Be Done." Editorial. October 23, 1898, II, 6.

———. "Will Bring Both Back." November 25, 1897, 2.

———. "Will Get Their Money." October 25, 1898, 3.

———. "Without Ceremony." October 12, 1898, 8.

THE COURSE OF TRUE LOVE, ETC.

Louisville Commercial. "I Want 'You, Ma Honey.'" February 5, 1897, 5.

———. "Marry or Stay in Jail." February 9, 1897, 1.

———. "Miller Now a Benedict." February 10, 1897, 1.

———. "On Trial: Racy Seduction Case." February 4, 1897, 8.

———. "Said 'I Am Innocent.'" February 6, 1897, 3.

———. "Will You Be My Valentine?" February 7, 1897, 5.

Louisville Courier-Journal. "Married in Jail." February 10, 1897, 8.

———. "The Miller Case." February 6, 1897, 8.

———. "One Year for Charles J. Miller." February 9, 1897, 8.

———. "Salacious Testimony." February 5, 1897, 7.

———. "Still Dragging." February 7, 1897, Section I, 8.

Louisville Times. "Miller Marries the Girl." February 9, 1897, 1.

———. "Warning Was Not Heeded." February 4, 1897, 5.

STRIKING A BLOW FOR THE WORKINGMAN

Louisville Courier-Journal. "Affecting Meeting of Condemned Man and Brother." October 16, 1904, I, 5.

———. "Affirms Decision." February 2, 1905, 5.

———. "Attended Funeral in Respect to Colleague." July 12, 1903, II, 3.

———. "Clemency Sought for George Warner." April 30, 1905, I, 9.

———. "Continues Warner Case for Defense." December 1, 1903, 10.

———. "Dead." July 8, 1903, 2.

———. "Deep Feeling Expressed at Death." July 9, 1903, 12.

———. "Defends Old Man." August 23, 1904, 8.

———. "Delay Inquest into Warner's Mental Condition." May 22, 1905, 2.

———. "Delay May Be Sought by…Warner." November 30, 1903, 7.

———. "The End Wished for by George B. Warner." May 27, 1905, 7.

———. "Extension of Time Granted." March 4, 1905, 2.

———. "Foreman of Warner Jury Refuses to Sign Petition." April 10, 1905, 3.

———. "Funeral Today." July 10, 1903, 5.

———. "George B. Warner." May 3, 1910, 6.

———. "George B. Warner Makes Escape." October 24, 1905, 1.

———. "George B. Warner on Way to Hopkinsville Asylum." April 27, 1910, 10.

———. "George B. Warner to Be Taken to Insane Asylum." May 2, 1910, 2.

———. "George Warner's Son Dies in Butte, Mont." February 28, 1906, 10.

———. "George Warner Will Hang First in New Jail." February 11, 1905, 12.

———. "Governor Is Asked for Requisition Papers." April 20, 1910, 14.

———. "Grief Killed Him." October 6, 1903, 2.

———. "Guard Dismissed." July 20, 1910, 4.

———. "Hangs May 19." April 1, 1905, 1.

———. "Hope Gone." May 17, 1905, 10.

———. "How Murder Is Encouraged." Editorial. November 26, 1910, 6.

———. "Impending Doom." May 16, 1904, 2.

———. "Indictment…Claimed to Be Defective." October 2, 1903, 12.

———. "Inquest Today as to George Warner's Sanity." May 18, 1905, 3.

———. "Inquiry from Warner." July 14, 1903, 7.

———. "Insanity Is George B. Warner's Plea." February 5, 1904, 6.

———. "Is Insane." May 28, 1905, I, 1+.

———. "Is Warner Insane?" May 14, 1905, III, 1.

———. "Large Reward." November 11, 1905, 3.

———. "Leeds' Slayer Under Arrest." April 19, 1910, 7.

———. "Life Sentence in Penitentiary Hangs Over Warner's Head." April 20, 1910, 8.

———. "Mrs. Warner Arrives to Attend Husband." July 12, 1903, I, 7.

———. "Mrs. Warner Here." March 8, 1905, 5.

———. "Mrs. Warner Says She Will Not Go to Frankfort." March 9, 1905, 10.

———. "Murder Verdict of Coroner's Jury." July 14, 1903, 12.

———. "Must Hang." February 7, 1904, II, 4.

———. "Must Hang." March 26, 1905, I, 5.

———. "Must Hang." May 12, 1905, 10.

———. "Nervous Following Experiences of Eventful Day." May 20, 1905, 12.

———. "Nightmare Prophetic of R. Lee Suter's Tragic End." July 9, 1904, 8.

———. "Nothing Heard from George B. Warner." October 25, 1905, 5.

———. "Not Worried." February 8, 1904, 10.

———. "Off for Montana." April 21, 1910, 3.

———. "On Trial." February 4, 1904, 10.

———. "Out of Danger." July 11, 1903, 2.

———. "Physicians Disagree as to Warner's Mental Condition." February 6, 1904, 7.

———. "Placed in Jail." July 24, 1903, 10.

———. "Prominent Doctors to Examine George B. Warner." May 24, 1905, 5.

———. "Punished by Conscience." Editorial. April 20, 1910, 6.

———. "Rehearing Asked." March 2, 1905, 5.

———. "Reward for Warner." November 11, 1905, 10.

———. "Sad Scenes at Funeral." July 11, 1903, 14.

———. "Seek to Save Warner." May 21, 1905, III, 7.

———. "Sees Husband." August 1, 1903, 14.

———. "Shot Down." July 7, 1903, 1+.

———. "Six Men in County Jail Under Sentence of Death." February 22, 1904, 10.

———. "Slayer of Pulaski Leeds Taken to Hopkinsville." May 4, 1910, 6.

———. "Slayer of Pulaski Leeds Will Be Called to Account." February 1, 1904, 10.

———. "To Ask Governor to Interfere." March 7, 1905, 10.

———. "To Hold Inquest Into Warner's Sanity." May 5, 1910, 5.

———. "'To the Sheriff' Warrant for Van Dalsen's Death Addressed." January 12, 1906, 7.

———. "Twenty Thousand…Have Signed Petition." April 7, 1905, 10.

———. "Veins Opened." October 15, 1904, 12.

———. "Want New Trials." February 28, 1904, II, 2.

———. "Warner Back in Louisville." May 1, 1910, IV, 8.

———. "Warner Committee Will Not Go to Frankfort." May 15, 1905, 7.

———. "Warner Escapes." July 2, 1910, 4.

———. "Warner Gets Another Chance to Save His Neck." May 19, 1905, 1+.

———. "Warner Improving Rapidly." July 20, 1903, 10.

———. "Warner Is Indicted for Murder." October 1, 1903, 10.

———. "Warner Murder Case Tomorrow." November 29, 1903, II, 2.

———. "Warner Must Die on the Gallows Friday." May 16, 1905, 3.

———. "Warner Sentenced." March 20, 1904, II, 3.

———. "Warner Taken to Asylum in Hopkinsville." June 2, 1905, 14.

———. "Warner Trial." February 3, 1904, 6.

About the Author

K even McQueen was born in Madison County, Kentucky. He is an instructor in the Department of English at Eastern Kentucky University and the author of twelve books of history, folklore, true crime and biography, mostly about Kentucky. He spends his free time pondering the meaning of existence and eating corn dogs.

Visit us at
www.historypress.net